The Making of a European Economist

WITHDRAWN
UTSA LIBRARIES

ALSO FROM EDWARD ELGAR

Educating Economists
The Teagle Discussion on Re-evaluating the Undergraduate Economics Major

Edited by **David Colander**, *Christian A. Johnson Distinguished Professor of Economics, Middlebury College, USA and* **KimMarie McGoldrick**, *Professor of Economics, University of Richmond, USA*

'This volume is an excellent outcome of an American Economic Association Committee for Economic Education project aimed at advancing the teaching of economics within a liberal arts context. Dave Colander and KimMarie McGoldrick assembled a most able panel of contributors for this effort that includes dialogue on what should be taught, how it should be taught, and how that teaching and learning should be assessed and rewarded. To the editors' credit, they have not attempted to dictate policy but to stimulate debate on the topics. This volume is a must read for anyone seriously interested in the teaching of economics at the tertiary level.'
– William E. Becker, Indiana University, USA

The economics major is a central part of a college education. Is that economics major doing what it is meant to do? And if not, how should it be changed? This book provides a provocative discussion of the economics major by many of the leaders in US economic education. It questions issues such as whether the disciplinary nature of undergraduate education is squeezing out the 'big-think' questions, and replacing them with 'little-think' questions, and whether we should change graduate training of economists to better prepare them to be teachers, rather than researchers.

November 2009   c272pp
Hardback 978 1 84844 579 6
Paperback 978 1 84844 580 2

The Making of a European Economist

David Colander

Christian A. Johnson Distinguished Professor of Economics, Middlebury College, USA

Edward Elgar
Cheltenham, UK • Northampton, MA, USA

© David Colander 2009

All rights reserved. No part of this publication may be reproduced, stored in a retrieval system or transmitted in any form or by any means, electronic, mechanical or photocopying, recording, or otherwise without the prior permission of the publisher.

Published by
Edward Elgar Publishing Limited
The Lypiatts
15 Lansdown Road
Cheltenham
Glos GL50 2JA
UK

Edward Elgar Publishing, Inc.
William Pratt House
9 Dewey Court
Northampton, Massachusetts 01060
USA

A catalogue record for this book
is available from the British Library

Library of Congress Control Number: 2009928614

Mixed Sources
Product group from well-managed
forests and other controlled sources
www.fsc.org Cert no. SA-COC-1565
© 1996 Forest Stewardship Council

ISBN 978 1 84844 639 7 (cased)
ISBN 978 1 84844 641 0 (paperback)

Printed and bound by MPG Books Group, UK

Library
University of Texas
at San Antonio

Contents

Tables

Preface

This book reports the results of a survey of students at global European graduate programs in economics and interviews at six of them. European economics is especially interesting at this time because of the changes that are currently going on there in response to the EU's Common Educational Policy. The book provides students' views of the ongoing changes and the difficulties these changes entail. It consists of an introductory chapter and a chapter summarizing the survey results and explaining the changes going on, three chapters reporting the qualitative survey results, six chapters of interviews with the students, and a final chapter drawing broader policy implications from the study.

Acknowledgements

Many people have made this book possible. First there is the Christian A. Johnson Foundation which has made it possible for me to do research outside the standard approach and to follow issues that are interesting. The Foundation's commitment to liberal arts education is unbending. Second, there is Middlebury College which, as a liberal arts college, encourages a wider range of research than most universities do. Together, they made this project possible.

Once I decided to do the project, I relied heavily on friends and contacts at various universities throughout Europe for information and help in distributing the questionnaire and reminding students to fill it out. The leadership of the EDP (European Doctoral Program) and ENTER (European Network for Training in Economic Research) consortiums were especially helpful as were the department chairs and department administrators at the various schools. I thank them all.

A non inclusive list of some of the people who were especially helpful include Marta Araque, Angela Baldassarre, Emanuela Boem, Amelie Constant, Jacques Dreze, Vincenzo Galasso, Fabrizio Germano, Andreas Haufler, Omar Licandro, David Madden, Patrick Pintus, John Sutton, Shlomo Weber, Philippe Weil, and Mark Wilbor. I thank them all, along with many others who helped, but whose name I, unfortunately, did not record. I would also like to thank *Kyklos* where the information in Chapter 2 was first presented in a 2008 article entitled "The Making of a European Economist" (*Kyklos*, **61**(2)). It is used with permission.

Having collected all the material, I had to analyze it, transcribe the interviews and edit all the material. A number of people at Middlebury College helped me in this and I would especially like to thank Helen Reiff, who helped with editing the interviews, and Jessica Weise who helped with analyzing data.

After I put the manuscript together, I turned it over to the people at Edward Elgar who did a masterful job of transforming it into a final manuscript. I would especially like to thank Jo Betteridge and Suzanne Mursell.

Finally, and most of all, I want to thank the graduate economics students at all the schools for filling out the survey and for agreeing to be interviewed. This is their story.

PART 1

Introduction

1. Introduction

I am an economist watcher. By that I mean that I follow what economists do, not in any deep sense of studying the formal methodology of economists, but simply observing, thinking about what happens, and writing about it. One of the most important aspects of economics that I focus on is the making of an economist. The reason this subject is important is that people are not born as economists; they are "produced" by universities that take student raw material and transform it into "economists."

Over the last 20 years, I have explored the graduate economics education production process in the United States through a series of surveys and interviews of students at top US schools (Colander and Klamer, 1987; Colander, 2006, 2007). In this book, I use that same approach to consider graduate education at a subset of top European graduate economics programs that have designed, or are in the process of designing, their programs to be similar to US programs. I call these programs "global economic programs," by which I mean that they are designed to be similar to top programs throughout the globe, and they see themselves as training economists in the same way as do other "global programs."

Typically, these global programs are designed to mimic US-style programs, and my first inclination was to call these programs US-style programs. I decided against that because economics has gone global, and there is nothing particularly US focused in modern global economics. By that I mean that US programs have a large number of non-US students (60–70 percent at top programs), and that the style of graduate training done in the US is extending throughout the globe. (Japan is the one major country that does not seem to be in the process of changing.)

Because of the internal pressure in Europe, brought about in part by the Common Educational Policy and the Bologna Accord, for other European programs to become "global programs," these global European programs are of special interest. They are the forerunners of the change that will be occurring in the teaching of graduate economics throughout the world. Given the pressures for change that European programs are experiencing, if before, as suggested by some commentators in a *Kyklos* symposium on European Economics (1995) there had been a separate "European economics," now it is doubtful that there is, and in the future it is almost certain that there will be no separate European economics. There will simply be a global economics, some of which will be done in Europe, some of which is done in the US, and some that is done elsewhere.

I have serious misgivings about this movement of European economics to mimic US programs. My previous books on the US economics profession (Klamer and Colander, 1990; Colander, 2006) highlighted serious problems with the US style of teaching graduate economics. Thus, it is not surprising that I am concerned about the wholesale importing of these methods into Europe, because doing so imports those problems into European programs. This is not to argue that academic European economics programs are not in need of change. They need serious reform. This book is written to influence that reform by getting them to recognize the problems with US-style graduate economics education, and to think more creatively than they have about the reforms that they are instituting. My goal is to get European schools to adopt the good parts of US graduate education—the professionalism and the incentives to work—while avoiding the bad parts—the far too strong focus on training students to write journal articles as opposed to solving real-world problems, and the lack of training and respect given to hands-on applied policy work. If they do that, the geographic center of gravity of global economics will shift from the US to Europe.

The book supplements earlier work on graduate education in Europe (Frey et al., 2007) and reports the results of a survey and interviews I did with European graduate students at these schools. The book (1) provides a profile of European graduate economics students at some top global schools in Europe; (2) considers the degree to which training at these European schools differs from US training; (3) offers some insights into the differences that exist among some top European programs in economics; and (4) provides a glimpse of the views that the students have of economics and of the training they are receiving. In the conclusion I discuss my concerns with the reforms that are currently underway in European economics.

The remainder of the book is organized as follows. Chapter 2 provides a summary of the survey results from respondents primarily at the London School of Economics (LSE), Stockholm School of Economics, Universität Bonn, Université Catholique de Louvain, Belgium, and Universitat Pompeu Fabra, Barcelona, and discusses those results. Chapters 3–5 provide further qualitative results of the survey, giving a sampling of student responses to what it means to be a successful economist, what characteristics put an economist on the fast track, and what students like and dislike about graduate work in economics. Chapters 6–11 present interviews with graduate students in economics at the LSE, the Stockholm School of Economics, the Université Catholique de Louvain, and Universitat Pompeu Fabra

(UPF), Università Bocconi, Milan and Oxford University. These interviews provide the context for the survey results, and give the reader insight into what those results mean.

The book concludes with an essay that explores some of the issues that came up in the interviews. It proposes a radically different way of thinking about and financing economists' research—one that gives credit for hands-on research rather than biasing the incentive system toward hands-off research. It does this by making economists' research subject to market pressures.

I have little expectation that my radical reforms will be implemented any time soon. But I hope that thinking about the alternative method of funding research that I propose gets readers to think about what we want out of the majority of academic economists, and how the training they receive can enhance those skills that we want economists to have. In doing so, I hope that the concluding chapter provides a different way of thinking about how to "make an economist," and how to think about reform of European graduate economics programs. I will have succeeded if the book provides a counterbalance to, what seems to me, an obsessive concern about rankings and output metrics based on quality-weighted journal article output that I find over in Europe, and moves the discussion of reform to how to change the incentives in European graduate programs in a way that builds on their strengths, rather than how the reforms can get them to mimic US programs.

2.   The making of a global European economist: survey results summary[1]

Back in the 1980s, Arjo Klamer and I had a radical idea. To understand what is going on in the profession, why not do a survey? That sounds reasonable to most people, but back then, that was not something that economists did. For an economist, it just wasn't a permissible allowable method of collecting data or of understanding how something works. (When I went to a program to distribute the survey, I was asked by a top economist whether I had left the profession.) Surveys are a bit more acceptable today, as are interviews, but they are still not used enough. For example, Truman Bewley's courageous book (Bewley, 1999) gets nowhere near the respect it deserves, but the use of the techniques is a bit more common, and doesn't bring about the same reactions as it did then.

Arjo's and my book (Klamer and Colander, 1990) became well known in the profession and led to the establishment of an American Economic Association (AEA) commission to study the graduate school training. The "COGEE" Commission (Krueger et al., 1991) came to similar, although more nuanced, conclusions to ours. However, neither had any effect on US graduate economic education. More recently, I redid the survey at US schools (Colander, 2006, 2007) and found that in the past decades, graduate economics education had changed. The positive change is that the training had become more empirical; the negative change is that it had become more focused on preparing students to be "efficient journal article writers," which made it less focused on preparing students to be good economists.

The idea to extend my consideration of graduate economics education to Europe came from suggestions of European economists who had seen my study of US economists and who believed that, given the changes that are ongoing in European economics, it would be interesting to see the differences between European student answers and US student answers. The idea was to provide some insight into where the integration has occurred and where differences still exist. So in 2005, I started the study, and arranged to do surveys and interviews with students at a variety of European schools. This chapter reports the results of a survey.

The survey was conducted in the fall of 2005 and the spring of 2006. I contacted students in a variety of ways. First I handed out surveys at graduate economics conferences at which I spoke. Second, I contacted directors of ENTER (European Network for Training in Economic Research) and EDP (European Doctoral Program) consortia, and asked them to send an e-mail to students in their program, with a link to the online survey. (These consortia are groups of schools that allow students to take courses at other schools in the consortium as part of their education. They offer a way for students to be exposed to different professors and different schools.) Third, I contacted friends at various European graduate economics programs and asked them to distribute an e-mail request to students in their program. Fourth, I went to graduate program websites that listed student e-mail addresses, and sent students an e-mail asking them to participate. Responses were limited to one per e-mail address. There was no way of assuring the randomness of responses, which opens the possibility for various biases; this means that the results should only be seen as suggestive, not as definitive.

In total, there were 270 respondents from 15 different programs, although not all students answered all questions. Five schools, London School of Economics, Stockholm School of Economics, Universität Bonn, Université Catholique de Louvain, and Universitat Pompeu Fabra, had more than 20 replies, and I limit my cross-school comparisons to these schools. The distribution of responses by year was: 1st: 23.5 percent; 2nd: 19.5 percent; 3rd: 31.1 percent; 4th: 14.7 percent; 5th: 11.2 percent. Of those who answered, 79 percent stated that they were in an ENTER or EDP consortium school.

To make the results comparable with the US results, I used the same survey questions I had used in the US. There were a few changes and additional questions in the European survey compared with my study of the US graduate economics education process. Additional questions concerned students' views of two consortia, ENTER and EDP, and the perceived cost to students of using English as the lingua franca of economics. Changes in questions from the US survey include slight changes of wording that were suggested by pre-survey respondents to account for different terminological usage of the same terms in Europe and the United States. When I compare the European and US results, I note these changes. A final change is that in this survey I switched to an online version of the survey from a paper version that I used in the United States.[2]

THE RISE OF GLOBAL ECONOMICS IN EUROPE

European economics is especially interesting to study at this time because of the changes that are currently taking place with the development of the

Common European Educational Policy. Whereas previously, European economists were in large part a collection of rather disparate German, French, Italian, Dutch, British, and so on, economists who were primarily trained in their home country in programs that reflected the distinct traditions of their country, over the last 20 years there has been a concerted attempt by some leaders in the European economics community to develop a more standardized European economics profession that competes favorably with the US economics profession, which is a leader in global economics training.

This emerging European economics profession sees itself as transcending borders; its lingua franca is English both in teaching and in scholarly communications. Generally, as its metric of success, it uses quality-weighted journal publications and citations, the same metric used by most US programs.[3] The changes occurring in European economics are not without their critics (see, for example, Kolm, 1988), but even those who oppose the changes see change as inevitable, and many see it on balance as a positive change.[4] Frey and Eichenberger (1992, 1993) call this "the inevitable consequence of the widening of the market for academic economists" and say that the change "cannot be reversed by exhortations or wishful thinking."

The structure of this chapter is as follows: First, after a brief profile of the students, I present the quantitative results of the survey and contrast those results with the results of my recent US survey. Then I briefly consider some comparisons in survey results among schools. Finally, I give my interpretation of the results and discuss some of the issues the results raise.

PROFILE OF THE STUDENTS

The average age of a European graduate student in the survey is 27.5 years, which is slightly older than the 26-year age of the students in my US survey. Women make up 30 percent of my European respondents, which compares closely to the 29 percent in my US survey. As was the case with US students, a majority of the European students do not go into graduate school directly, but instead have a variety of jobs beforehand. Some of these jobs are related to economics, but also include military service and jobs in the business sector to a greater degree than was the case with students in US schools. The large majority of the students (75 percent) majored in economics as undergraduates; 7 percent majored in mathematics, and 22 percent have other degrees. (Some students had double majors.) Nearly two-thirds of students considered attending an alternate school.

Of these students, 38 percent looked at schools in the United States. They chose not to go to the United States for a variety of reasons: financial, denial of admittance to the school they wanted to attend, distance, deadlines, and social considerations.

Most students surveyed come from upper-middle-class families, and while there is a wide range of educational backgrounds of the parents, a majority of the students have at least one parent who had attained a university degree. Nearly 70 percent of students received scholarships and/or grants, and only 4 percent were totally self-financed. One large difference between the US and European surveys is in the origin of students. In my US survey, 70 percent of the graduate students were non-US citizens. In Europe, only 17 percent were non-European. Within the European context, 57 percent of the students came from a country different from the country in which they are studying. The percentages differed widely by school; for example, 10 percent of the London School of Economics respondents were natives of the UK, while 76 percent of the Universität Bonn respondents were German natives. Only 1 respondent was an American.

When asked to rank their graduate program with other graduate programs in Europe, the large majority (80 percent) of respondents ranked their university in the top ten in Europe; 21 percent ranked their university in the top two schools in Europe, and 5.5 percent ranked their program in the top ten in the world.

When asked how they would classify their political beliefs, 43 percent classified themselves as center, 39 percent as liberal, and 7 percent as conservative. (Six percent listed "other"; 5 percent classified themselves as indifferent.) Because of the difference in the terminology in the question, and the different interpretations of the terms in the United States and in Europe, it is difficult to compare these results with the US results where I gave students different options: conservative, moderate, and liberal. However, in the United States, 16 percent of the students classified themselves as conservative, 24 percent as moderate, and 49 percent as liberal. My sense is that, in the United States, there is a slightly larger group of students falling in the conservative range than in Europe, but overall in both the United States and Europe the majority of students fall to the center left of the political spectrum.

To explore whether graduate training influenced students' political views, I asked whether their political views had changed while in school. A large majority, 87 percent, said their views did not change in graduate school. Of the 13 percent who said their views had changed, 72 percent moved to the right and 27 percent moved to the left. Thus, there seems to be a slight shift toward conservativism in the students, which is similar to my results for the United States.

QUANTITATIVE RESULTS OF THE SURVEY

Table 2.1 compares student interest by area (organized by degree of great interest) for European students and contrasts my findings with those for the United States.

As you can see, in Europe, micro theory attracts the most interest, followed by econometrics and economic development. In comparison with the United States the two differences that stand out most are that European students seem to be more interested in econometrics and political economy than are students in the United States, whereas students in the United States show a greater interest in applied micro areas such as urban, law and economics, public finance, and labor.

One of the results of the US survey that received much comment in the popular press concerned the skills that students considered important for success. Table 2.2 compares the perceptions of success that the European economists reported, and contrasts them with the results for US students.

The results here show some differences, but not enormous ones. Overall, European economics graduate students saw almost all these skills as being more important than did US economics graduate students. The largest relative differences were that the European students tended to see a knowledge of economics literature and a knowledge of the economy as more important than did US students. I suspect that this difference reflects the difference in what many of these European graduate students will do in their likely jobs, compared with what most of the US graduates in my US

Table 2.1   Interests of students by area

Interests	European Graduate Students (%)	US Graduate Students (%)
Micro theory	43	35
Econometrics	40	22
Economic development	37	39
Political economy	35	24
Macro theory	35	33
Labor	25	32
Money and banking	21	21
Public finance	20	24
International trade	20	19
History of thought	15	9
Comp. ec. systems	12	9
Law and economics	9	15
Urban	6	11

Table 2.2 Perceptions of success

Criteria	Very Important		Moderately Important		Unimportant		Don't Know	
	European (%)	US (%)	European (%)	US (%)	European (%)	US (%)	European (%)	US (%)
Being smart in the sense that they are good at problem-solving	61	51	34	38	6	7	0	2
Being interested in, and good at, empirical research	38	30	51	52	9	12	2	4
Excellence in mathematics	40	30	51	52	9	14	0	3
Being very knowledgeable about one particular field	35	35	48	42	14	15	3	7
Ability to make connections with prominent professors	30	33	54	40	11	19	5	7
A broad knowledge of the economics literature	16	11	53	44	28	35	3	8
A thorough knowledge of the economy	16	9	39	24	42	51	4	15

study will do in their likely jobs. At the top schools I surveyed in the United States, the students are being groomed almost unidimensionally to become academic research economists. As I will discuss below, that is less so for students in European programs, who were more likely to be moving into more policy-related jobs that value a broader knowledge of the economy more highly than is the case with US students.[5]

Table 2.3 presents the results of a question about how stressful students found the programs. The interesting result here is that, almost across the

Table 2.3   Elements of stress—US vs. European students

Stressful Elements	Very Stressful		Stressful		Moderately Stressful		Not Stressful	
	European (%)	US (%)	European (%)	US (%)	European (%)	US (%)	European (%)	US (%)
Course work	17	33	29	31	35	25	19	9
Your financial situation	10	8	14	11	25	33	50	46
Relationship with faculty	5	9	13	24	32	33	50	32
Relationship with students	1	1	4	10	13	25	82	64
Doing the mathematics	6	11	18	21	37	31	39	36
Finding a dissertation topic	16	28	22	32	38	20	24	18
Maintaining a meaningful life outside school	9	21	16	22	31	29	44	26
Conflict between course content and your interests	7	15	24	18	45	34	25	32

board, US students found graduate school to be more stressful than did European students. Student comments in interviews reinforced this result, and I sensed a more laid-back attitude of students in European programs than I did of students of US programs. One European student captured the sense the European students have of the US when he said, "Some friends of mine, who are studying in the United States, say that it is much more competitive, and the environment is a bit awful."[6]

Table 2.4 presents both the current views of the European students on a number of propositions about economics, and those they held prior to entering graduate school, and contrasts those views with the current and prior views of students in US graduate student programs.

Table 2.4   Current vs. earlier perspectives on economics

Perspectives	Current View Strongly Agree		View Before Entering Graduate School Strongly Agree	
	European (%)	US (%)	European (%)	US (%)
Economics is relevant for today[a]	34	44	37	37
Economists agree on the fundamental issues	9	9	11	11
We can draw a sharp line between positive and normative economics	9	12	10	15
Learning neoclassical economics is learning a set of tools	41	36	23	26
Economics is the most scientific of the social sciences	36	50	34	46

Note: [a]The US survey specified "neoclassical economics." Because the term "neoclassical" proved ambiguous for many students in the US study—they did not know what it meant—the European study specified "economics." Thus, the responses to this question are not directly comparable as between the United States and Europe. Still, since neoclassical economics is a subcategory of economics, it would seem that the response rate for European economists in a comparable question would have been even lower.

Looking first at the changing views of European economists, the largest change in their views occurred in their perception that learning neoclassical economics is learning a set of tools; it increased from 23 percent of the students strongly agreeing to 41 percent strongly agreeing with that proposition. There were only slight changes in the current and prior views of the students at European programs on other statements.

Contrasting US and European views and changes, we see that students in US programs currently view economics as more relevant and more scientific than do students in European programs. However, US students came in believing more strongly that learning economics was learning a set of tools, but currently they were slightly less likely than European students to strongly agree to that proposition. The other area where there seems to be a difference is in the views about economics being the most scientific: the US figures were higher than the European, both before and after.

Table 2.5   Importance of economic assumptions[a]

Assumptions	Very Important		Important in Some Cases		Unimportant		No Strong Opinion	
	European (%)	US (%)	European (%)	US (%)	European (%)	US (%)	European (%)	US (%)
The assumption of rational behavior	40	51	53	43	5	5	2	1
Economic behavior according to conventions	14	9	55	55	12	17	20	19
The rational expectations hypothesis	25	25	55	58	15	13	6	4
Imperfect competition	49	37	44	58	2	3	5	2
Price rigidities	25	14	61	65	8	11	16	10
Cost mark-up pricing	16	5	50	47	9	18	25	30

Note: [a]In the US survey the first statement read, "The neoclassical assumption of rational behavior." In the European survey the first statement read, "The assumption of rational behavior," so the comparison here is not direct.

Table 2.5 presents the responses to a question on the importance of various economic assumptions.

The largest differences here show up in the bottom three rows—reporting views on imperfect competition, cost mark-up, and price rigidities. In general, it seems that students in European programs see assumptions reflecting institutional constraints and reality as more important than do students in US programs. (These results are consistent with the earlier results reported in Table 2.2 that showed that students in European programs believed that having a knowledge of economic institutions was more important than students in US programs believed it was.)

Table 2.6 reports the views of European students on economic policy issues and contrasts them with US results. What stands out about this table is the similarity of results of European and American student views

Table 2.6 Views on policy issues

Views	No Opinion		Disagree		Agree With Reservations		Agree	
	European (%)	US (%)	European (%)	US (%)	European (%)	US (%)	European (%)	US (%)
Fiscal policy can be an effective tool in a stabilization policy	12	9	9	12	59	58	21	21
Central banks should maintain a constant growth of the money supply	21	22	42	50	28	22	9	7
The distribution of income in developed nations should be more equal	4	9	18	18	43	41	35	32
A minimum wage increases unemployment among young and unskilled workers	11	7	25	23	38	38	26	33
Tariffs and import quotas reduce general economic welfare	7	3	9	7	43	39	42	51
Inflation is primarily a monetary phenomenon	15	14	27	20	38	33	20	34
The market system tends to discriminate against women	11	11	31	47	34	28	25	14

on economic policy. I found much more difference among schools in the US than I found between US schools considered as a whole and European schools considered as a whole.

OTHER FINDINGS

The development of consortia of European programs is a novel and potentially fruitful idea to take advantages of specialization and economies of scale, so I was interested in how the students felt about them. Of the 166 students who responded to this question, 14 percent rated their experience with the consortia as highly positive, 34 percent rated it positive, 51 percent said they were indifferent, and 1 percent had a negative experience. In interviews, I was told that many students prefer to go to the United States to study for a year, an option that many of the schools offer, and that there were limitations on movements of students among consortium schools. So while the consortium idea remains novel and potentially fruitful, at this point it has not developed enough to significantly influence the students' education. My sense is that, for the most part, the consortia are not central to most students' education.

A key element of graduate education of the European programs that I studied, compared with the many other European programs, is that the language of instruction in all the programs I considered is English. For non-English speakers, this could be a serious cost, so I asked a question about whether the students felt that their productivity was reduced by English being the language of economics. Table 2.7 reports the results by native language. The cost was lower than I thought it would be, with 67 percent of the respondents saying that it reduced productivity by 5 percent or less.[7] It seemed to be more costly to French and Italian native speakers than it was to German or Spanish native speakers.

In the interviews, the students reaffirmed this view that the costs were not very great. A typical response of a student is the following: "Actually, I started learning economics in a third language, Spanish, and am more comfortable in that language than in English. In any case, I'm more effective writing in Spanish than in English. The mathematics doesn't matter what language you are writing in."

CROSS-SCHOOL COMPARISON

Another question I was interested in was how much variation there was in views across schools. Table 2.8 reports the students answering "very stress-

Table 2.7   The cost of using English

Cost	Italian (%)	Spanish (%)	French (%)	German (%)	Total[a] (%)
No effect at all	13	50	12	59.3	37
Reduces your productivity by less than 5%	30	17	24	27.8	30
Reduces your productivity by between 5% and 10%	40	25	35	5.6	21
Reduces your productivity by 10% to 20%	11	8	17	5.6	8
Reduces your productivity by more than 20%	5	0	2	1.9	4

Note: [a] "Total" refers to the total of students who listed one of the standard non-English European languages as native. Even though British schools are included, there were only 8 percent native English speakers in the survey.

Table 2.8   Comparative views on stress

Criteria	Bonn (%)	LSE (%)	Stockholm (%)	Louvain (%)	UPF (%)	Total (%)
Course work	25	22	8	10	14	17
Your financial situation	0	17	8	10	5	10
Relationships with faculty	10	6	0	5	0	5
Relationships with students	0	6	0	0	0	1
Doing the mathematics	0	6	4	14	0	6
Finding a dissertation topic	10	33	12	19	19	16
Maintaining a meaningful life outside graduate school	0	22	8	14	5	9
Conflict between course content and your interests	0	6	8	14	10	7

Table 2.9   Views on economic policy: students strongly agreeing

Views	Bonn (%)	LSE (%)	Stockholm (%)	Louvain (%)	Pomp (%)	Total for all Schools (%)
Fiscal policy can be an effective tool in a stabilization policy	6	16	4	37	17	21
Central banks should maintain a constant growth of the money supply	17	0	4	17	6	9
The distribution of income in developed nations should be more equal	17	44	21	47	22	35
A minimum wage increases unemployment among young and unskilled workers	28	16	17	21	61	26
Tariffs and import quotas reduce general economic welfare	50	50	40	44	50	42
Inflation is primarily a monetary phenomenon	22	22	16	28	28	20
Wage–price controls should be used to control inflation	0	0	0	6	0	3

ful" to a question asking them to rank the various aspects of graduate school as very stressful, stressful, or moderately stressful, for those schools in which there were 20 respondents or more.

In course work stress, Bonn and LSE stood out, and, overall, LSE exhibits the most stress, which is probably because LSE is most like US schools, and in worldwide rankings generally is ranked higher than the other schools in the survey.

Table 2.9 reports the students' views on policy by school. Specifically, it reports the percentage of students who agreed without reservation to a variety of statements about policy.

While there are some differences here, these differences on policy views are smaller than are the differences that I found among US schools, where there was a wide variation among students' views on policy.[8] This suggests that, on average, European schools are less diverse on policy than are US schools.

DISCUSSION OF THE RESULTS

The above results give one a reasonably good picture of graduate economics education at the subset of European schools that see themselves as "global European programs," as opposed to those who see themselves as country-specific European programs. To a large degree, the results of the survey suggest that these European schools have succeeded in making their programs very similar to US programs, and have eliminated much of the country-specific traditions. The students seem relatively content, and there is no strong dissatisfaction with economics or with their graduate programs. The students liked the rigor of the programs and want a "training that is competitive with the US training." When asked an open-ended question about whether graduate programs in Europe should be structured similarly to US programs, a majority of students responded yes, they should be. When asked whether the research agendas of US and European economists should differ, the large majority said no. A representative response to my question about whether European programs should be designed after US programs was: "Yes, because the US system has become the standard of value, and for good reason!"

What the students almost universally found most objectionable about the old-style traditional country-specific economics programs was the rigid autocratic structure of many of those programs. The following comments are typical: "Many European universities still have a rigid structure, with students having to attach themselves closely to a professor in order to get a PhD; this is obviously not productive"; and "The organizational structure for the US system is more efficient in teaching students modern economics; the European system is too rigid." Because of that rigidity in the European programs, most students agreed that change was needed.

Despite the agreement about the need for change, it is not clear to many of the students that the path towards change that the schools are following is the ideal path. Specifically, numerous students questioned whether the current approach of essentially mimicking the US programs is the best way for the change to occur. Students noted a number of problems with structuring the programs after the US programs, especially for schools that are not yet fully integrated into the US job market for economists. While the students agree that the US institutional structure had advantages, they were hesitant about Europe just copying that structure rather than learning from it and designing a system that incorporates the best of both the traditional European and US institutional structures.

Consider the response of one student:

> On the one hand the US system proves to be more productive when it comes to quality of the students that are sent into the job markets. But the question is: why is it so? Is it because the general structure of the US system is such that it allows researchers to produce the top research? Or [is it because of] the virtues of US society, like tough competition, are the driver behind it? Neither theme is being pursued in Europe: as the Europeans are not used to paying big money for the education and are not used to competing hard. Hence, why should we copy the US system? Let's try to stick to ours with some corrections, like enhancing the ability of researchers to concentrate on research and not on bureaucratic stuff, give flexibility to universities in administrating their money, and so on.

Another student suggested more creativity in designing European programs: "Until now, European graduate schools just copied the US model; they should try to be more creative and think of new ways of graduate education (for example, stronger links to policy institutes, ministries, companies, and so on, to promote applied research besides the theoretical work)."

In thinking about which path European economics programs should follow, in my view, three points should be kept in mind:

1. The traditional European system does some things right.
2. The European academic economics institutional structure and job markets are quite different from the US structure and markets.
3. The US system has its own set of problems.

Let me briefly discuss each of these.

The Traditional European System Does Some Things Right

US economics programs rank higher than European programs in journal output (Neary et al., 2003). That fact, however, does not necessarily mean that the US system of graduate economics training is better than the European system of training. Economists' output is not only journal publications; economists also teach economics, play a role in public debates through their more popular writings, advise government and policymakers, and do research that is not published in journals. Any ranking that hopes to compare European and US graduate programs in economics must take all aspects of economists' output into consideration. When one does so, one finds that there is just too little hard data to make a firm comparison.

In part because European academic researchers have not had the strong focus on journal publication that US researchers have had, European programs have provided training better suited to other aspects of economists' output. As Bruno Frey and Reiner Eichenberger (1992, 1993) have pointed out, European economists have tended to take a more active part in hands-on policy; they have been more likely to become public intellectuals, and concentrate their training on undergraduate teaching. Because they didn't have to focus on journal publication, they could focus on other aspects of economics, such as service to government; applied policy work in institutes, which often guides policy but seldom gets published; and in providing solid undergraduate teaching to students, which is one of the reasons why European undergraduate training is generally considered more rigorous than US undergraduate training. When all these roles are considered, my estimate is that, at most, 20 percent of economists' contribution to society is captured by journal articles.[9]

Because the US system promotion metric within universities is almost totally based on journal publication research, and the European system is not, my general impression is that the traditional European graduate economics programs do far better on these other aspects of economists' output than does the US system. Even in terms of important research ideas, it is not clear to me that the United States ranks so far ahead of Europe as the studies summarized by Neary et al. (2003) suggest. The reason is that journal publications are not necessarily a good proxy for important research ideas, which make up the ultimate research output. As Tönu Puu (2006) argues, research is not necessarily related to development of ideas, and the fact that European economists tend to place less emphasis on journal publications than do US-based economists does not necessarily imply that they are not working on research, or that they are less creative. As he states, it might just signify that they are "more choosy" about what they regarded as being significant enough to merit publication (Puu, 2006, pp. 31–2). His observation rings true to my sense about the publishing environments in Europe and the United States, although it has been changing in the last 20 years, as Europe has followed the US in its focus on journal publication metrics.

The reality is that much of what is published in journals in the United States is published primarily because it is in US academic economists' interest to publish as much as possible. Journal publication per capita by economists at US policy institutes, government, or business is far less. But that does not necessarily mean that these non-academic economists are not doing research, or are not making an important contribution to society; it just means that they are focusing on a different aspect of economists' output.

When I asked graduate students in US programs about the possibility that the incentive toward publishing was driving much of the publication output in the United States, almost all students agreed that it was. For example, one student stated, "In a top journal like the *Quarterly Journal of Economics* I'd say at least half [of the articles] are useless. Probably 20 percent are useful and the rest are unclear." The other students in the interview concurred. When considering research output, it is important to remember that what are important are ideas, and in my interaction with European economists I have found that Europe has been an incubator of new ideas in economics, and that there are pockets of excellence in the development of new research ideas that demonstrate a breadth of knowledge and interest that has almost been lost in the United States.

For example, European economists are on the forefront of work in econophysics, complexity analysis, cointegrated vector autoregression analysis, non-linear dynamics, experimental economics, heterogeneous-agent macro, agent-based modeling, general-to-specific econometrics, and a variety of other areas. Some of these areas may well make up the foundation of the economics of the future. That work can thrive in Europe better than it can in the United States, in part because the incentives toward publishing in Europe are different than in the United States. It would be a shame to lose that incubator aspect of European economics in an attempt to compete with the United States on a flawed metric of research output.

A third aspect of training that the European system seems to be doing right is its method of undergraduate teaching as a preparation for graduate school. It is generally agreed by both United States students and European students that the European undergraduate students are technically much better prepared than are US students, whose technical undergraduate education is much weaker. A possible reason for that is that US incentives for professors go strongly toward graduate training; undergraduate training is often a poor stepchild that gets little focus by professors in programs offering graduate degrees.

There are a variety of reasons for this greater focus in the US on graduate education, but an important one is US economists' focus on published research. In the United States, graduate courses, including core courses, often involve faculty teaching their latest research to the students in order to take advantage of economies of scope in teaching and research. They teach what they are doing. This is one of the major reasons that the core courses generally don't provide context for the research or any discussion of why the research being taught to students in the core is important. Similarly, graduate training in the US often provides students with no introduction to research that has been done, or is being done, by others on the same topic. If professors spend time teaching work outside the specific work they are doing, it would detract from their own journal publication research. My sense is that the competitive pressure to publish is so strong in many graduate schools, especially those not in the top ten, that teaching in many schools has become contributive to journal publication research, not derivative from it.

Teaching only professors' current research might be useful training for graduate students if the sole goal of that teaching were to create future journal contributors. But in my view, the goal is broader—the goal is to create well-read students who understand where their research fits into economic understanding. US graduate education in economics does not strive toward that goal. Because, until recently, the incentives have differed for European economists, traditional European education has been more focused on teaching, especially undergraduate teaching, and one would like to make sure that this strength is not lost in the transition.[10]

The European and US Institutional Structures and Job Markets Differ

Even if one does not share my concern about the value of much journal publication research, there is still a serious question about designing the European system of graduate economics training after the US system with its focus on journal publication. The concern is that the institutional structures the European graduates are being sent into differ significantly from the US institutional structure. The US style of training has been designed to fit the US institutional structure, which has a unified job market that uses journal publication as its primary metric. That is not the case in Europe, where a unified job market is only evolving. This led to two different reactions. The first was from students who were aware of the global job market. They saw that market as a US-dominated market, and saw themselves at a competitive disadvantage. They consistently stated in interviews that their degrees were undervalued within that global market.

Other students in programs that were not yet as fully globalized had a lack of preparedness for the job market they would be entering.[11] In the interviews at one school I asked about what they will do when they finish their studies, and all the students laughed. I asked why. One student responded:

> I'm laughing because when I finished I had no clue about the job market. I don't know how the job market works here. We had no clue about how the US market works for professors until we had a lecture about how it works there with interviews with several universities. We saw it as another world. I don't know how it works in Europe.

They all then agree that they are very worried.

I next asked about their job strategies. In response to that question,

US students generally had carefully delineated plans. Many continental European students didn't. One student responded:

> I'm sending some applications now, but these are general applications. Until you have a PhD, there is little sense in sending anything else. Here in Europe, personal relationships mean much more in determining who gets what job. In Italy, that is definitely the case. If you are outside the system, it is unlikely that you will get a job.

The students all noted that there were no job placement officers there, and that "all the work about job searches we have to do ourselves. At best, you might get some help from a professor who knows someone who knows someone else." The interview concluded with the question: "So is it fair to say that they graduate students and then leave you on your own?" and the responses were, in unison, "Yes, definitely."

These responses suggest that there is a serious transition problem for students when the European programs adopt the US structure. Programs in the early stage of transition are not preparing students for the job market they will be entering, and programs that have more fully changed find that their degrees tend to be undervalued.

The US System Has its Own Set of Problems

When Arjo Klamer and I did our initial study of top US graduate economic programs, we did not find anything that was not generally known. We simply provided some quantitative measures of what active US economists knew—that US graduate programs had become highly technical, and were more concerned with theory for the sake of theory than they were to adding to our understanding of economic affairs. Because of that focus on theory, graduate programs were losing their connection to institutions and economic literature, and leading students to believe that empirical work was an add-on, and not something that was taken seriously by researchers. That's why our findings struck a sympathetic chord among many in the profession, and why our findings led to the establishment of an AEA Commission (COGEE) to reconsider graduate economics education.

The COGEE recommendations (Krueger et al., 1991) included the following: that "reasonable requirements in mathematics, statistics, and economics be established"; that "core courses be taught in a way that can balance breadth and depth, with sufficient attention to applications and real-world linkages to encourage students themselves to start applying the concepts"; that "the core should be regarded as a departmental 'public good' and its content be the concern of the entire department"; that "field courses should attempt to include more empirical applications"; that "greater attention should be given to writing and communication skills"; that "efforts should be made to ease the transition from course work to dissertation"; and that "more differentiation should exist among departments."

COGEE's specific recommendations fell on deaf ears (Colander, 1998), and graduate economics education at top US schools continued on much as before. No attempt was made to make the core content the concern of the entire department, and the core focused less and less on breadth, and more and more on technical depth; history of thought and economic history requirements were eliminated from many of the programs, and students wanting to go into policy work or into undergraduate teaching were generally seen as second-class citizens.

Nonetheless, as I reported in Colander (2006, 2007), over the last 20 years, students in US programs have become more satisfied than they had been previously. The reasons were two-fold. First, students entering the program have better information about the nature of graduate economics education than they did in the 1980s. They know what they were getting into and have self-selected to go into that type of program.[12] Second, what economists do has changed, and as it did, dissertation work and field courses have become more closely tied into what the students will be doing once they move on to academic jobs at graduate programs. In the past 20 years, economics research has become much more empirically sophisticated; today students have much better technical tools available to them to answer the questions than students 20 years ago had. This has led to a decrease in theory unrelated to reality, and an increase in an integrated empirical/theoretical approach. The mathematics used has changed more to applied mathematics, and economists well-trained in these technical areas are in high demand in business. In the 1980s, there was little concern about a theoretical microeconomist moving into business; today, there is. Research has also opened up. Allowable assumptions for modeling have become much less rigid, opening up a wide range of avenues for research, such as behavioral economics and experimental economics.

These changes in economics have made students in US programs much happier about their field courses. The changes have made doing economic research more exciting for students since the technical work they are learning in micro theory and econometrics is much more useful in answering real-world questions than it was in the 1980s. (Macro has gone the other way, and in my latest study, the majority of US students were highly dissatisfied with the macro core (Colander, 2007).)

The US programs are also doing a better job at integrating the students into academic research; US graduate economics students start writing journal articles early on in their graduate education, and they feel that they are learning the skills they need to write those journal articles. In many ways, what the US programs do is to create highly efficient "journal article writers," which is the skill they will need to succeed in a US academic institutional environment.

However, the match between training and needed skills is far less adequate for students going on into applied policy institutes, undergraduate teaching, or hands-on policy work (Stock and Hansen, 2004). At the top schools in the United States that I interviewed, such concerns are disregarded by the faculty; they are blunt about the fact that their interest is in producing academic researchers. So while the top US schools are doing a good job preparing academic research economists, they are far less effective in training applied policy research economists.

Hands-on vs. Hands-off Research

As noted by Frey and Eichenberger (1993), a larger percentage of European graduate students continue on to work in policy institutes or governments or move into academic jobs that are local in nature. These economists do research but the type of research they do is what might be called "hands-on applied policy" by which I mean research that directly advises government on how to solve a particular problem. Such research can be very useful, but it generally is not the type of research that leads to publication in an economics journal. Hands-on research often involves judgment and integration of broader issues into the analysis than does hands-off applied policy. Such hands-on applied research can be contrasted with "hands-off applied research," which is only indirectly related to policy. Hands-off applied research is what fills most journals and the primary direct consumers of hands-off applied research are other researchers, not policy-makers. A large percentage of true hands-on research is seldom published in an academic journal, but is instead embodied in reports, memos, and verbal advice.

Both these types of applied economic research are important, but the US graduate economics education training is geared only toward the former, whereas the traditional European system provides training in both. For an academic in the United States that type of hands-off applied research has little payoff, since it leads to little in the way of journal publications, which has become the almost single metric of US economists' output, even in many of the regional central bank branches.[13] If Europe moves to the US metric, it may well undermine that contribution that academic European economists are making to hands-off applied research, leaving such research to other professions.[14]

I will return to these themes at the conclusion of the book. In the next two sections, I let the students speak and report their qualitative views on the program. Part 2 gives a sampling of students' qualitative responses to the survey questions and Part 3 gives the interviews with the students.

NOTES

1. Parts of this chapter were earlier presented in Colander (2008).
2. In reporting the results economists may note that I do not report statistical significance results—and present just the figures. This is by design. I make no claim that the survey is, or could be, formally scientific, and reporting statistical significance would make it look more scientific than it is. The push for the appearance of scientific certainty is something that pervades modern empirical work in economics, when in fact, often in economic empirical analysis all one has is nuanced evidence that is better judged with common sense significance.
3. There have been a variety of ranking studies, some of which have been sponsored by the European Economics Association (EEA), that use the journal publication metric as the sole determining metric for ranking. See Neary et al. (2003).
4. See, for instance, Portes (1987), Kirman and Dahl (1994), and Salmon (1995).
5. A recent similar study of German economists (Frey et al., 2007) asked a similar question: what makes a good economist? In response 76 percent said being knowledgeable about a particular field was very important; 59 percent said empirical skills were very important; 54 percent said a knowledge of economic literature was very important; 48 percent said a knowledge of the economy was very important; 45 percent said being good at problem-solving was very important; 25 percent said mathematical knowledge was very important, and 7 percent said that connections were very important.
6. This difference is not because of the higher probability of students failing the program. Except for Chicago, all the schools that I surveyed in the United States had very few students being asked to leave the program.
7. I should note, however, that this estimate of the cost of English is an underestimate of the total cost to non-native English speakers in all European economics programs since these students have self-selected into a program that is taught in English. My suspicion is that the perceived costs to non-native speakers of using English as the language of economics is much higher in other programs.
8. The variations in US student views across schools are narrowing, however, and my latest findings show far less variation than there was in the first study when students at schools took completely different positions on these policy issues (see Colander, 2007).
9. Clearly, any judgment is subjective, but my 20 percent estimate for journal article output is, I believe, defensible. Teaching is clearly an important element of economists' output; in a survey of over 1100 US professors teaching principles of economics in the United States, 53 percent attributed between 50–75 percent of economists' contribution to society as resulting from teaching, and 10 percent attributed 75–100 percent to teaching. Another key element of economists' output is their contribution to policy debates and applied work that is never published, but instead is an input into making decisions. Journal articles are generally not timely enough to play a role in such decisions. Business and government economists in the United States publish little, but play important roles in determining how economics is translated into policy.
10. Even if European incentives focused on journal publication as much as US incentives, Europeans would still find themselves at a disadvantage, since US journals are ranked higher, and they tend to focus on US rather than European data, and reflect ties with US scholars. Journals are conversations, and to publish in a journal, it helps to be part of that conversation. It is much harder for Europeans to be part of the conversation than it is for US economists at the top set of schools.

11. The knowledge of the job market varied among schools, and in the last few years broader job markets have begun to develop in Europe (Inomics.com; Jobs.ac.uk). The top European schools tend to hire in the US job market, to encourage their best students to take part in that US job market, and to take jobs in the US if offered one. Information about job markets relevant for European students has increased significantly. See, for example, House et al. (2002) and John Cawley (2004).
12. The better knowledge of what the programs are is one of the reasons why the top US programs have only about 30 percent US students.
13. Whereas earlier, banks used to give little emphasis to publication, today, banks are creating research groups whose output is judged by peer-reviewed article publication, regardless of the article's connection to monetary policy. For example, the Boston Federal Reserve Bank has a group focused on behavioral economics.
14. There is certainly such concern among some European economists. In a survey of German economists (Frey et al., 2007) only 5 percent saw the US as a good model for reform of German universities. They saw other European systems as better models, even though these programs are also in the process of changing to be more like the US.

PART 2

Qualitative results of the survey

3. What makes a successful economist?

Having an idea of what students are aiming for provides insight into the way they approach the world. Thus, in my survey I asked three questions relating to student aims. The first was a simple question—which economist, living or dead, do you admire most? The answers to this question were varied, but tended to emphasize living economists over dead ones. The most admired economist was Paul Krugman, followed by J.M. Keynes, Joseph Stiglitz, Amartya Sen, and Adam Smith. All these were economists who have combined contributions in theory with contributions in public policy, so it seems that it is that combination that students find most attractive.

The second and third questions were more open-ended questions. They were: what is your idea of a successful economist and what puts an economist on the fast track?[1] I recognize that these questions can be interpreted in many ways. I specifically left the questions ambiguous because I was interested in how students would interpret them. Would they recognize the ambiguity, or would they interpret the questions in a certain way, as if that were the natural way to interpret them? The way a question is interpreted is often as telling as the actual answer. For example, if students interpret "successful" as involving journal publication, they were more integrated into the current system than if they questioned the relevance of much of the economic literature as being of interest to policy and society. Similarly with the question about fast track. I wanted to see if students would interpret it as an unambiguous positive for someone to be on the fast track, or would they see a potential conflict between success in the field, and success as an economist? As you will see, the answers vary—the students are not a homogeneous group. The students I interviewed reflect a variety of quite different views.

What is your idea of a successful economist?
- Someone whose work has impact (for example, J. Nash).
- Creative, open-minded, strong common sense ability to reduce problems to their essentials.
- Addressing relevant questions, not an epsilon-variation of the theory. Using simple but effective models to highlight certain mechanisms.
- Being able to formulate questions that are relevant in actual economies and answering these questions in an abstract framework.

31

- Good at problem-finding and solving; demonstrates a thorough knowledge of the economy.
- Strong intuition, observing the world, able to translate ideas into models and then able to solve models well.
- More experience in real life.
- Learn to think like an economist, be able to write down complicated models, but don't get lost in them, be able to convince people of your ideas, seek connections to the real world and try to change it.
- Asks good questions, is skillful at finding answers.
- Publishing in good journals, exploiting a good idea only once and not five times.
- Being able to transmit abstract concepts to the broad public in simple terms.
- One who influences thinking and also practical application of economics by governments.
- One who approaches the question with no bias; uses good economic theory and applied tools to provide an understanding of expected outcomes; is able to communicate outcomes to non-economists; and utilizes other disciplines where this makes sense, for example, the physical sciences in applications such as the environment.
- Perceived by society: one who publishes a lot. Perceived by me: one who is able to make the non-obvious obvious; one who can pass that knowledge on to other professional economists, to students, and to the rest of the world.
- Has a permanent research-oriented job. Plays a role in both academia and policy advice. Can explain complex issues clearly in press or even TV.
- Someone who improves theory and empirical findings such that economics performs a better job at helping us to understand reality and make well-informed decisions. Those findings should be published and have a large impact.
- Mix of empirical and theoretical skills, policy-relevant research, and good communications skills.
- A long list of publications in top journals, professor in a top university, supervising plenty of graduate students writing joint papers (that, too, get published in top journals), good performer and teacher, giving keynote speeches at good conferences, government asks him/her for policy advice.
- Highly published. Can succeed in writing about economics to a broad audience. Advisor to governments.
- One who actually produces relevant research.
- An economist whose contributions are respected in the profession and are accepted and published in leading journals.
- Provides research useful for society.
- Develop a tool which people frequently use. An example is the input–output analysis by Leontief.
- Hard working, enthusiastic, and creative; has good analytical skills.
- Being able to do great research that helps policy-making.
- Points us to a better position to understand the real world.
- The way things *Are* now, it suffices with publishing a lot in academic journals and getting tenure. As to how things *Should* be, I think the profession should also reward those who try to communicate to a broader audience.
- Good (in academic terms) research, the ability to make it known by the non-specialists, and political relevance.
- Creative approaches to answer important questions. Mathematical complexity

should not be encouraged beyond what necessity requires, and then the person needs the ability to write well and market the idea properly.

- Someone who does rigorous work of relevance to policy.
- Proficiency in different fields, knowledge of recent developments and literature, ability to communicate and expose ideas.
- Someone who is able to understand—and why not to predict—the evolution of the important economic variables, together with their political implications. Furthermore, someone who then gives his insights directly to policy-makers.
- If by successful you mean "good," then: an economist who has excellent technical modeling skills, theoretically and/or empirically, and at the same time has an excellent understanding of when and how models are applicable to real economic questions, and of the limits of such models. If successful means respected by the profession, then publication in top journals seems to be both necessary and sufficient today.
- I believe a successful economist should be able to provide good analysis of human behavior, both theoretically and empirically.
- Safeguard the prosperity of the world and help the poor countries.
- For academic: make theoretical advance with respect to the reality; convey knowledge successfully to students; diffuse economic ideas to public. For those working in professional or practical fields: apply economic theory or technique to real problems.
- Influencing politics, convincing politicians.
- Being modern in thinking and following economic processes swiftly.
- Smart, delivering excellent and simple ideas, good in mathematics, taking into account empirics and history and forgetting about policy implications, hard working.
- Publishing on different issues.
- A successful economist is someone able to identify and understand the main forces and effects underlying an empirical phenomenon or a political decision.
- Knows a lot about various fields of economics; knows theory but can apply it to the real world; can explain even complicated models in simple words; never stops learning; never stops being curious.
- A successful economist must be a curious guy who wants to discover something new studying something old.
- Someone who can think creatively and is able to apply theory to practice.
- Being a professor in a good university; writing papers in top journals; being prestigious.
- Doing good research on topics that really matter (economic development, environmental issues).
- Sharp economic analyst of problems of relevance (and not of problems only of relevance in highly imaginary nonsensical worlds).
- Has some widely cited papers, with implications for policy.
- Someone who can take a simple question about why we behave as we do—for example, "Why doesn't capital flow to poor countries?"—and come up with a model and a good empirical test. The ability to clearly define the question you are asking, telling us why it is important and getting to grips with how this "question" may have come about.
- An intellectual person who understands and researches the financial, sociological, and possibly psychological interactions among individuals in a framework that is somehow depicted and restricted by concepts like preferences,

money, birth, death, time, place, and so on, and who models and tests this framework using justified assumptions. This would be the basic economist. A successful one would be the one who is listened to and who actually makes a difference.

- Open mind, sense for innovation, patience.
- My realistic idea is someone who publishes papers in top journals. Nothing else matters at all.
- Good mathematical and analytical skills, having good connections to publish by knowing well-known professors, studying at a renowned university and this must be a top ten.
- Highly intuitive, being able to see connections between different fields of economic study, excellent researcher, excellent writer.
- The one who can develop good ideas and model them in good papers, and also the one who is able to explain them to the rest of the world in plain words. Good researcher but also good teacher.
- Theorist.
- Being able to show what we could do better in the economy; provide valuable solutions to problems that are so complex that others do not see how to solve them (see problems from the bird's eye view).
- Creative mind. Technical/mathematical competency is not enough to make someone a good economist. A good economic intuition is a must.
- Patient, careful, smart.
- Somebody who publishes in good journals and is able to explain his or her ideas to non-economists.
- Able to propose solutions to problems that occur in reality, analysing relevant questions (as opposed to participating in purely academic debates).
- Someone who successfully combines theoretical and empirical methods to solve a practical issue.
- High capability of recycling himself once the wind of theory has taken a twist; for instance, being able to write something about R&D and growth when it is a "hot" topic for the growth theorist; being able to write something about contract theory when it has come into fashion for the international trade literature; becoming an econometrician when the *AER* [*American Economic Review*] expressly requires an econometric section for each publication. Of course, the fact that the new fashion comes up against its own principles must not be an issue!!
- A person who is able to look at the economic reality and find and use the appropriate knowledge in economic science in order to explain it and try to solve problems and find new ways to improve, correct, or disclaim the current state of the science.
- You should be more: a mathematician and have an important place on the politician scene.
- A philosopher in research and a problem-solver in the reality; being critical (not cynical!) to his/her field.
- Managing to get some good advice through to politics/practitioners. Contributing to better policy and better understanding of economics.
- New, original, and relevant ideas; strong communication skills.
- Contributes to the stock of knowledge about society (including the production of new concepts/ways of looking at society), which directly or indirectly improves the ability of the public to take individual and collective action.

- An economist who has become famous with the theory he/she believes to be the right one to describe the world.
- One who is very happy with his job.
- Capable of leaving his mark of his thought in the shared view, successful in explaining phenomena never explained before.
- Excellent research, but is also very good at teaching and communicating personal ideas to others.
- A person whose works are the basis for other scientists. A person who solves problems.
- Able to explain social evolution.
- Someone who is able to contribute strongly to a deeper understanding of the economic system.
- A person who knows the real world, succeeds in understanding how it works and the causal relations behind it, finds out how to exploit these relations in order to let people live better lives.
- Being able to give alternative views on specific political problems, being heard in politics and becoming widely known for these abilities.
- Brilliant research.
- Popular, smart, powerful.
- A person with common sense who can make some positive contribution to economic policy.
- A successful economist is first of all a good mathematician. He specializes in one (or a few) particular field[s] and applies particular techniques with great accuracy. What I would really like to learn is a real knowledge of economic problems.
- Makes relevant contributions in a policy sense, or theoretical ones that allow others to do so. Creates "useful" knowledge. This means connection to real issues. Good teaching, too.
- Professor at a good university, academic publications in prestigious journals, and authority in the public debate in his field.
- An economist with an established position, both in scientific and academic fields (publications in reference journals and being a professor in a major institution).
- Ability to bring ideas/methods from other fields into his own area. Ability to abstract from traditional approaches and offer new solutions and perspectives.
- To be able to conduct societal-relevant research that is academically good.
- Doing new inventive stuff that creates new fields (for example, information economics, psychological and behavioral economics).
- A social scientist, in the meaning of both "social" and "scientist," combining institutional knowledge, common sense, sound theory, and rigorous empirical analysis to enhance our understanding of society.
- Open-minded, practices self-expression and interdisciplinary approach. Plus all the rest: brilliant, good at model building, knows much about both empirical and theoretical work.
- Someone like Krugman, who is good at both writing theoretical papers and applied analysis.
- Link directly or indirectly knowledge and insights to phenomena in the real world. Ability to communicate and teach others the insights that he reaches. Of course, standard characteristics: smart, hard-working, innovative, and so on.

- Thorough analysis of problems that are relevant today. Ability to communicate those findings.
- Innovative, questions established result, can connect reality with theory.
- Interested in actual economic behavior/data. Would try to model/test observed behavior/data.
- One whose work is influential on future research and policy-making and has passed the test of time.
- Like Keynes, outstanding in both theory and practice.
- She or he is able to convince people outside the profession that she or he has something valuable to say about the pressing issues that society faces.

What puts an economist on the fast track?
- Being able to anticipate "hot topics" and write in such areas. Also, being able to market oneself well through conference attendance, and so on.
- Personality traits, such as intrinsic motivation and self-discipline.
- Ability to capture economically relevant questions within the most simple framework (relates to the first characteristic listed above).
- Creativity generally.
- Creativity: being good at developing ideas, enthusiasm about one's own ideas, not afraid of starting work before seeing where it leads.
- Creativity in the skill to find nice topics—very important.
- Being good in receiving help from professors, hints and potential questions for research (this is half of the deal at least); networking.
- Never feel disappointed by failure of research ideas. Never feel intimidated from talking to professors. Both characteristics speed up the progress of a PhD student conducting research.
- Creativity and the skill to find nice topics, very important.
- For graduate students: choose a halfway wide field of research; if working on a niche, it'd better be a new one nobody has ever worked on; cover more than one area with your research; be interested.
- Ability to work without questioning too much. Economic tools are important, many economic results are not (and can give you a feeling of incompleteness if you think about them too much).
- Asking good questions.
- Rigor and capacity for hard work. Demonstrate an ability to pick a "neat" topic for a paper sometimes, even if it isn't the most important topic.
- A skilled economist can approach an allocation problem with a systematic framework. This allows the economist to understand the inter-relationships between the environment (endowments), the institution (the allocation mechanism), and the outcomes.
- Being successful sycophants and establishing a good relationship with the faculty are all-important.
- Combining productivity with quality.
- Open-mindedness to other fields besides economics.
- Diligence.
- Fast track to go where? Depends on where you wanna go. My answers assume that you mean to perform well in academia but would significantly change if the goal were something else; for example, to go into policy advice.

- A crucial characteristic: enter a top university, talk to the top professors. For a given quality of research, these two make a potentially large difference.
- Attendance at seminars/conferences, that is, networking, also important.
- Ability to memorize a lot of facts and figures and retain them for a long time after learning them.
- Being focused. Know what you want to do and do it. Self-discipline and time management.
- Asking the right questions, reducing complexity.
- You have to find a professor, who promotes you, who likes your ideas and your approach. Alternatively, you have to be adaptable to the approach and interests of a specific professor if you already have a special topic and special approach for your research. It is very important to select the "right" graduate school, where your ideas can grow and will find support.
- Being ambitious, able to concentrate, and particularly able to organize and motivate oneself.
- Being creative, having imagination, being passionate, being patient: does not look for results but for achievement.
- Ability to identify current fashions and get into "good" schools.
- Being good at asking the right questions.
- I think it depends on your research area. For myself: my topic is inventory management and therefore I need some math and empirical research is an important part. If your topic is, for example, game theory, then math is very important, but empirical research is often not that important.
- Being able to find a field of research that has not been previously considered.
- Depends on in which area of economics you plan to work. A good game theorist might not know much about the economics itself (theory or empirics). A good applied economist might not need to excel in (abstract) mathematics.
- Patience—research is a long-run commitment.
- Working hard.
- Being a good presenter—nobody wants to have to read your papers. You must be able to tell what you are doing in a precise yet entertaining way.
- "Solving" a problem is to answer intelligently a question. To do so someone must at least get an idea of the empirical relevance of what one is trying to understand (even if he is trying to do "mathematical economics" . . . I think). Otherwise I don't think the work is important. (I have several friends who represent their countries in Olympic games of maths. They are not the best economists of their class even though they are at the top US schools. I think that John Hicks said that "It is very difficult to give a good answer to a bad question." I agree.
- I think economists have to have a kind of ability of making some fresh ideas in their specialized field.
- Having a genuine interest in social issues and economic problems of the world.
- Understanding the importance of assumptions in a model and their implications for model results.
- Luck.
- It is all maths!
- Good communication and interpersonal skills.
- Study hard.
- The most important traits are not specified above explicitly. They are creativity and discipline.

NOTE

1. These questions were follow-up questions to Table 2.2 in Chapter 2, which listed various characteristics and asked students which ones put them on the fast track.

4. What students like and dislike about graduate work in economics

Two further questions I asked students was what they liked and disliked about graduate school. The hope here was to see if any themes were emphasized, and to sample the general feeling of the students about their studies and the program. As with the other questions, the questions were open-ended by design to see what aspects students chose to mention. A few themes did show up. Specifically, the students ranked freedom to study what they wanted high on the list. The students also liked the quality of the teaching, and the entire process of graduate school—learning a set of tools that they believe will be useful in their careers and in finding answers to economic questions.

The dislikes were, of course, there, but the lists of dislikes were well within the range of dislikes that I would expect to get from any large collection of students when I ask them about programs they were in. These "dislikes" often focused on bureaucratic problems at specific schools or on the lack of supervision by faculty. In general, I interpret the combination of likes and dislikes as a positive statement about the way economics is structured and done at these programs. They could do it better, but the students are calling for changes at the margin, not for wholesale changes.

What do students like about graduate work in economics?
- The flexibility to pursue my own academic interests in my own time.
- Being able to choose the items I want to study.
- In contrast to the traditional German way of doing your PhD as a professor's assistant, you have more flexibility concerning the choice of your topic, a stronger focus on international competitors, and the opportunity to stay abroad for one year. Furthermore—and probably the most important issue—a graduate school encourages cooperation among students and helps to build up a relation to faculty members.
- Great relationship with co-students.
- Interaction of students and professors, seminars offered, social networking, courses offered.
- Freedom to do my own research (within broad limits).
- Interaction with the other students, the offered courses, approachability of professors.
- Freedom to concentrate on my interests!
- Discussion with other young professors and students.

- Acquiring knowledge, discussions, meeting other graduate students.
- Getting in touch with other graduate students and professors; learning new facts and methods; pursuing my own ideas.
- That you are free to do research in whatever topic you like.
- Being part of a lively academic community.
- Exposure to high levels of scholarship and intellectual discourse as well as to diverse views about the solutions to very important problems in the world economy. There seems to be more respect for interdisciplinarity in European universities as well.
- Nothing.
- Environment (other doctoral students, seminars to exchange ideas, and so forth).
- Despite all the emphasis on methods, many of the questions in modern economics are intellectually quite stimulating. The flexibility and freedom of student life is very nice as well.
- The environment is rich in intellectual stimuli. I like the international atmosphere.
- As a PhD student I like to have the freedom to work on topics that I am interested in and to have time to read further into a topic if I want to. It's a privilege to not have to earn money.
- I have a strong feeling that the skills I'm learning will allow me to do meaningful work in my professional life.
- Rigor. Seminars in which there is a high level of participation by senior faculty members.
- The opportunity to get in touch with some of the most important research in my field of interest.
- The opportunity to work on what you are interested in and interact with many clever and interesting people.
- Learning a lot of tools.
- Doing high-quality research.
- Challenging. Intellectual freedom. The atmosphere of "ideas" in our research group (for example, seminars, meetings, lunch discussions, and so on).
- The range of topics, courses at research level.
- The mental training.
- The freedom to read and research any topic you want and to have open discussions with others.
- Opportunity to get closer contact with very interesting (and interested) and bright people. Having all the time in the world to think and try to answer interesting questions and being paid for that (although this ends up being quite stressful at the same time).
- Can get up when I like and have long naps.
- The rigorous thinking and some of the people I have met.
- Flexibility in the way you allocate your time. The fact you are, on average, surrounded by smart people. You can push your brain till it goes to the limit.
- The freedom to work.
- There are a diversified group of excellent researchers and professors.
- Many conferences and talks about up-to-date topics and the edge of research. Opportunity to discuss topics with fellow students, especially of higher years. Good administrative support.
- Provision of basic tools (mathematics and others).

- Freedom, course work, group feeling.
- Supported with all facilities you could need for study, lots of guest researchers, motivating atmosphere for study.
- The open atmosphere. You can go and talk to any professor and they will listen to you and help you.
- I like very much the opportunity to get in touch with different economic approaches in order to consider a major variety of points of view.
- Having the time to think thoroughly about one topic. Being able to interact with scholars from other institutions.
- Sharing information with students with different backgrounds; flexibility in courses and in research activities.
- Being able to do research on topic of my choice.
- Great environment; quality of other people enrolled in the program.
- Learning! And being with students who enjoy economics, not only students (as undergrad ones) who want a degree.
- Smart people around.
- I like that I can study what really interests me. In my previous career as a research analyst I never felt like I was being stretched and the work was repetitive. I enjoy UPF as the faculty are very supportive (although busy). I especially like the fact that courses generally come with the chance to write a small paper or project instead of an exam. At this level it is more appropriate and is good practice for the eventual writing of a thesis. The competitive spirit is a mixed blessing.
- Unfortunately, I think that the best feature of the school I am attending is its location. This is by far the side that I like the most. Other things would be that it is competitive, and hopefully has a good reputation.
- Studying, learning, meeting other students from different countries.
- The level of difficulty of the course work.
- Quality of teaching and faculty.
- Learning and studying economic problems; establishing networks of study and work.
- Faculty.
- Liberty to work on what and how I want.
- The academic environment; the fact that you have to study and read all the time and be up to date with things that happen in the world.
- Chance to explore ideas.
- You have a very intensive time and you learn a lot about advanced economics; especially you start to understand the deeper sense of economics.
- Freedom to do your own research.
- I am research-oriented and I aim to do a good PhD and join the academia.
- Being able to dive into more complex problems and analyzing them from more than just one standpoint; research writing.
- The freedom and the combination of studying, teaching, and doing research.
- Learning new knowledge and tools.
- Working in groups with other students instead of fighting alone; benefit from cooperation.
- I prefer doing this every day to working in a bank or any other company. I am able to do what I like most among all the things that are paid.
- Intellectual freedom.
- Mine in particular?—financial situation and office space. Accessibility of some faculty members.

- Opportunity for intellectual work.
- It's not clear to me yet.
- Share the same set of interests and problems with people in the same situation.
- The interaction with many colleagues and researchers from all kinds of different levels of education (PhD students, post-docs, senior faculty); the various ideas one is confronted with; the scientific environment.
- The opportunity to specialize and the time to acquire a set of tools that can help you to sell yourself in the market.
- Intellectual freedom.
- Satisfied and free atmosphere to do the research I am interested in.
- Deepening knowledge, experience in teaching and research, sharing the experience with similarly-minded colleagues.
- I can manage my life without too many stringent constraints.
- The friends; the time we have to think about a problem; and the democratic sense of life we get working in what we like, when we like, and how we like.
- Environment, professional approach.
- The diploma. To have courses with some respected professors.
- Challenging myself intellectually while being able to keep a flexible schedule.
- The opportunity of always learning something new about how actual economies work. In general, the intellectual environment, which could be better, but could also be much worse!
- Discussions with professors and other students; seminars; the large set of courses available: economic history & thought, ethics and economics.
- Being creative, being involved in stimulating discussions, thinking of real-world problems.
- Being your own "boss" perhaps. And the environment to challenge your intellect.
- Doing research.
- I've learned a lot of tools, especially the econometric techniques.
- Being paid for studying.
- The opportunity to spend one year abroad.
- Freedom of research topics.
- Trying to satisfy research curiosity.
- The debate about the different schools of thought (for example, macro is just the IS/LM model).
- Openness to different opinions and several research topics.
- Having time and money.
- Economics as a subject and tool of analysis on most social phenomena. Now I'm learning the tools better for future work.
- You open your mind, get in touch with smart people. Keep on enhancing your education. Way more exciting than working at a bank.
- The freedom to devote time and energy to a topic that interests me.
- Growing chances for cooperation with universities from abroad.
- Exciting research environment, competition, rigor.
- Its reputation.
- Motivating research environment.
- The freedom, flexibility, and intellectual challenge.
- The opportunity to conduct your own research and learning up to date methods.

- Feeling progress in my learning and understanding.
- Time for concentration.
- I like interesting and motivating professors.
- To solve problems. They expand my capacity to think and structure analysis.
- Opportunity to spend time thinking.
- Studying economics, discuss with people with same interests.
- Freedom to choose and explore research area; support of faculty and students.
- Doing something very serious.

What do students dislike about graduate work in economics?

- A little bit too short (three years); not enough information on mobility fellowships and on the following years.
- Being encouraged to talk to other members of the faculty may also lead to your adviser feeling less responsible.
- Availability of some professors.
- Peer pressure. Professors do not seem responsible for the students (you need to approach them beggar-like).
- Lack of guidance.
- Course work.
- Too many interesting fields and a tough choice when picking your thesis topic, which you are expected to stick with for the coming years.
- Feeling uninformed, unprofessional, being concerned about the time it takes to get something done.
- Doing compulsory course work in subjects you are not likely to do research in later on.
- Lack of commitment to the graduate program on the side of professors.
- Petty politics, the inward-looking nature of some academics, and occasionally poor organization.
- Some tension between those whose specialties are oriented toward modeling and mathematical formalism and those whose approaches are more empirical, historical, or inclusive of political and sociological analysis. However, this problem seems to be diminishing somewhat in some North American universities and was one of the main attractions of studying at a European university.
- The complete indifference of faculty members to what their students are doing, even to the point that they actually try to get rid of the students.
- The effect that competition can have on social relationships with other students.
- I dislike that my life is often dominated by school, especially when things go badly with research or when being on the academic job market. I also dislike to live "like a student," that is, not in my own apartment but rather in student accommodation.
- Not enough contact with professors; paranoid behavior of some students and professors, instead of fruitful discussions.
- Competition is sometimes so tough that it could undermine research and make some shy people very bad.
- Disorganized approach to teaching, yet high demands on quality of course work. Administrative chaos—PhD students get smallest level of support. This has been somewhat resolved at my school.
- Sometimes the days can be too repetitive.

- Constraints on leisure time and continual stress.
- The fracture between students and professors.
- Lack of professional approach from faculty and students.
- Lack of the mathematical and computational courses.
- The uneasy financial situation.
- The uncertainty of where I (and my peers) will end up. It's so hard to know (until the end) how you'll do on the job market, and so much rides on this. (Even the decision of whether to go into academia, or whether to work in the US or not, rides on how you think you'll do on the market.)
- Stress.
- Courses should be more research-oriented; faculty should give clear and motivating advice on the potentially fruitful research area.
- The loss of social life.
- As a graduate student it is sometimes hard to be taken seriously outside the university.
- Incapacity to disconnect from work. Research worries are present 365 days a year.
- Have to think too much.
- The disconnection from reality of some of my professors and co-students, and the fact that much of what gets studied in economics gets studied purely because of fashion and not because it has any intrinsic importance to the world.
- The scarcity of women who are both attractive and psychologically stable.
- Financial uncertainty. Some people are really presumptuous (even faculty, when you think that maturity should have already kicked in!).
- It can be isolating.
- Feelings of self-doubt inspired, relative lack of support.
- Very stressful sometimes.
- No clear structure to the day.
- The Italian way of organization. But it is tolerable in comparison with the general administrative environment in Italy. Lack of time to concern oneself with topics of own interest.
- Course work with no relation to subjects of interest.
- Especially during the first year it is relatively difficult to find faculty supporting students with their PhD-proposal preparation.
- The (mathematical) approach to economics, the content of courses and lectures, that modeling is the one and only useful and accepted way of economics, no connection to real-world problems.
- Low income.
- Once beyond the course work, there is no clear connection between effort and credit you get. This is a general problem of academic economics: much randomness enters the equation (access to data, quality of data, model closure may or may not work).
- Professors leave you on your own.
- Bureaucracy; unclear rules/requirements.
- The widespread academic "branleurism." Students do not care about economics; they care about getting a job and earning money. They [expletive deleted] whomever (supervisor, journal editor, and so on) in order to fulfill their objectives.
- Nothing.
- A lot of research is irrelevant.

- The pressure of finding a dissertation topic. As a second year, there is a lot of pressure to find a topic for your dissertation and I always worry about not being able to come up with something good. Finding a life outside graduate school is also a little difficult. Graduate school is a lot of work and as a foreigner who doesn't yet speak fantastic Spanish it can be hard to meet people outside grad school or pursue my outside interests.
- Pedant professors.
- That there's hardly any time to breathe between the various deadlines for assignments, problem sets, and exams.
- Some professors are not good at explaining concepts. They go too fast or assume we know stuff we do not. I am not sure to what extent problem sets are meaningful.
- Listening to paper presentations that are boring, beyond my immediate understanding, or both.
- Too few courses to choose.
- Myopia about what goes on outside of the academics.
- Not internationally diverse.
- Missing effort of professors in teaching and supervision.
- The life of a graduate student is a bit static. And sometimes it is quite frustrating with your research; you can work for one month and not see any results or realize that you've made a big mistake.
- Small number of assistant professors.
- Too little interaction in classes, or too many students there.
- Having to produce ideas.
- Since it's very intense, people, especially current and former students, put pressure on you by saying, "It's difficult"; "You are going out on weekends? How can you do that? You have to study." Moreover, I discovered that a lot of nerds are studying economics and it's difficult with them to go into a deeper and more meaningful and personal friendship.
- Pressure. Being so solitary. Doubts about yourself.
- I don't get many opportunities to talk with the faculty to find specific research interest and make future plans.
- Pressure of being thrown out.
- Too many tools, too little intuition.
- They do not apparently care about us. They rank us, so that there is competition among us.
- The current state of some computers, which have not been repaired yet.
- Study is stressful.
- High pressure, throwing away one year of life.
- The huge amount of work, little choice of supervisors for the dissertation, little support from the supervisor, limited scope of topics for which support is available from the faculty.
- Lack of collaboration.
- Problems with the financing; even the students that performed best during the first year have a hard time finding funding.
- It is very difficult either to maintain a meaningful life outside graduate school or to be very efficient as a researcher. I need to practice more.
- Having to do all that math on uninteresting subjects for two years, before I can deal with things I am really interested in.
- Lacking integration with faculty, lacking coordination between faculty members

concerning workload—faculty seems to think grad students are not working enough and need to be monitored.
- The first year is really tough.
- The distant link between the real world and problems studied in the academia.
- Professors after the start; professors who think math is sufficient for economics; economists who are only theorists or only empiricists; the academics market is a market full of singles; families are not welcome; arrogant people.
- Low efficiency in everyday work.
- Stress around exam period; some lack of pedagogical skills from teachers.
- "Negative competition" between the students.
- The excessive competition between the students and the stress of publishing.
- You cannot specialize in what you are really interested in from the very beginning of the course.
- Uncertainty about the future.
- The idea that without a bunch of formulas, your work won't look as serious as it could be. Also the fact that colleagues have their research on the tip of their tongue all day long, all days of the year.
- The program is very rigorous and stressful.
- Low flexibility in research topics.
- Living out of reality.
- Stressful; no more normal social activities.
- Too many courses, not possible to go in-depth in all of them. The fact that it is compulsory to take advanced courses in all main branches (econometrics, macro, micro). Moreover, it has been difficult for me to be working and studying at the same time. What is required from you as a teaching assistant and as a student is too vague.
- The lack of structure, of information about what's to be done, and what is to be done first.
- Silly formalization of otherwise obvious ideas. More in general the fact that we seem more concerned with putting in old formulas and known ideas than with looking for more satisfactory explanations about how market economies work today.
- Do you mean about my graduate school? To get a high mark for a lecture while I was unable (according to me) to make proper links with "the real world" but good enough with maths; no evaluation (of the excellence) in teaching (I am not sure this does exist now); no (at least structured) help in the placement of students after they receive their degrees.
- Stress, low pay, employment situation.
- Little interaction before starting research. No empirical courses or classes to deal with real-life issues; taking courses.
- Its closed-mindedness.
- The complete irrelevance of most of the "economic" things I've studied to understand economies.
- The struggle for signaling one's own ability.
- Little help by faculty; research is left to individual's initiative.
- Planning of internal courses.
- No teaching.
- There's too little focus on intuition and what economic analysis really is. You can pass exams without knowing what you really are doing, that is, just by having a good mathematical background.

- Uncertainty about the future.
- The course work. It is highly irrelevant, particularly considering students (such as me) with a Master's degree in economics.
- No PhD courses, weak scientific collaboration with other researchers.
- No specialization in the first year—lots of work in areas I'm not interested in.
- The infrastructure.
- Lack of financing (obsolete computers, small library, and so on).
- The race of top journal publications and the lack of joint work.
- I have to teach.
- The administrative work.
- Not easy to establish cooperation from other students and from professors.
- Hard to find the right dissertation topic.
- Prestige—people's skill seems to be less valued.
- Future job insecurity.
- The salary.
- Expectations!
- The emphasis on problem-solving as opposed to real thinking.
- Stressful. Insecure future.
- Nothing.
- Don't know. Perhaps the stress, but it comes with the seriousness I guess.
- The feeling of personal irrelevance.

5.   Are economists relevant?

In Chapter 2, I reported the numerical results to the question: do you consider the role that economists currently have in society relevant? Sixty-eight percent said yes, 9 percent said no, and 23 percent said they were uncertain. I then asked them to explain their answers. In this chapter I present their explanations. As you will see, there is a lot of variation in how students interpreted the question and in what they mean by "relevant." Specifically, relevant does not necessarily mean that the students see the "the economics profession's influence as positive." Students observe that economists influence policy-making in government, and are therefore relevant, but, for many of them, whether the policy truly improves people's lives remains in question.

Although the question asked if the role that economists currently have in society is relevant, many students answered by arguing for the relevance of economics as a field—but not for the relevance of current economists. By and large, students believe that economics is an extremely relevant and important social science that concerns all people and helps to elucidate human action. They are also optimistic about the contribution that economics could make to policy-making and to better government policy. However, many students were less sure about the direct contributions of economists to society. Specifically, a number of students voiced concerns about the inability of economists to communicate with a broad sector of the population, complaining that economists were too involved with complex theoretical work.

Explain why you think economists are relevant or not
- I toyed between Yes and Uncertain for this question. I tend to Yes because I believe that economists can inform policy and have a real impact on economic development, institutions, and so on. A degree of uncertainty stems from the following: (1) I feel that oftentimes economists conduct research in a vacuum—either without reference to real phenomena at all, or using some empirical regularity (at best) to motivate research that extends our knowledge in a relatively small way but cannot be refuted/confirmed. I am a theorist myself, but can see the limited application of much theoretical work. (2) The practical tools with which economists can have a real effect are somewhat limited and the relationship between the tools and outcomes is not clearly understood, often change over time, and may change when one tries to manipulate them! As such, the working of economics in practice is much cruder than the elegant mechanisms suggested by theory.

Empirical analysis on the other hand, though carried out far more effectively from a methodological standpoint in recent years, is still rife with spurious correlations that motivate theory, and so on. For example, the Grossman-Helpman [GH] lobbying political economy approach is used very widely and several empirical analyses are cited as support for the contributions framework. Recent work by Krishna et al. has shown that data confirming GH can be generated from a process with no political economy interactions at all! They build a model devoid of political economy components, with general assumptions; they simulated the model generating data, which they then used to run a regression in the Mitra et al. vein, which offered statistically significant support for GH, even though the data-generating process had no GH features whatsoever! There are many examples of this kind, but this is the most recent I have read. Empirical evidence motivates theory, which in turn motivates empirics, all stages of which may be subject to severe weaknesses, while in its entirety the research becomes part of the accepted body of economics "knowledge." So to summarize, I have my doubts about the degree of relevance of economists'/economics research to society because: (1) the link between the development of the academic literature and real applications is sometimes weak; (2) of the difficulties in refuting/confirming theories; (3) the incentive structures in place encourage economists to publish as much research as possible in the best possible journals. There is emphasis on volume and in my view far more work is published than is worth reading! There is much overspecialization and publishing for the sake of publishing rather than for the furthering of our understanding.

- Economists are relevant in the sense that their arguments are often heard in public debate. In Germany, the high unemployment rate is a fundamental issue in the public debate, so it is not surprising that economists are often asked to comment on labor market reform, and so on. However, although economists are asked their opinion, political decision-makers often choose not to follow the economists' advice. The best examples are the several blatant mistakes in economic policy that were made during the process of German reunification.

- Because I think that our current society is more moved by economic problems than before.

- As professionals: policy advice, consultants in firms, research, and teaching. In private: helping others (and oneself) to understand basic economic concepts in order to improve decisions and to assess political decisions (on a macro level).

- I think economists have an influence on politics and the public debate although sometimes not as much as they should have.

- Depends on the country. In the US the answer appears to be Yes. In Germany, the answer is clearly No in politics. Personally, I think economists' role is very relevant, but economists are not listened to very often; however, it is not easy to communicate theoretical results to practice.

- Explicitly or implicitly, the way people think about society is influenced by what economists argue.

- Most economists don't work in their own ivory tower. They do their research by combining practice and theory. Therefore, their contribution would have impact on practice.

- Economists understand some fundamental problems of our societies quite well. Conflicts of interest, hidden information, incentives, strategic interaction— these are areas economists understand and economists can help make society work better.

- Not what they know, but how they think.
- Economists are particularly well prepared for policy-defining positions.
- Economics is the painful elaboration of the obvious—as much as that can be useful, economists are useful.
- Relevant if they work at international institutions or the Fed and try to apply economic insights to "real-world problems." In general, economists working only academically, as long as they do not have a very high reputation (this is valid only for very few academics, who again are mostly involved in tackling "real-world problems"), have almost no real impact.
- Economists are always behind important decisions in a country. Political economics are always based on studies carried out by economists.
- Economic policy is very much influenced by economic research.
- People are not happier despite all economic theories.
- Economists can contribute enormously to the public debate on policy issues. They have tools that help us separate the cause and effect of things. Economists can quantify and understand the concept of opportunity costs. Economics is applicable to many circumstances (although not all, of course).
- Economists are trying to understand many important social phenomena using very scientific approaches in comparison with other social scientists. Such scientific approaches do contribute to our understanding, in a more rigorous way, of how the human society operates, such that researchers or policy-makers can more rigorously debate or examine these economic theories.
- Economics is definitely relevant to political society today but whether the role of economists per se is relevant is less clear.
- For macroeconomists: bad economic policy can really ruin a country—see, for example, Argentina.
- Economists have tools to conduct research that can plausibly aim to make claims on causality (I'm thinking about relatively modest things like program evaluation). This is rare among social scientists. Even more rare (good) economists think hard about what is causal and what is just correlation. I would also argue that (good) economists do not "know" their results before starting the research, while my impression of, say, political scientists is that they start from the answer they want. I also think that economists have quite a lot of weight in public debate.
- Economists have the most successful method for attempting to understand average human behavior.
- Because economics is everyday life.
- A restricted circle of scholars does policy-relevant research in a serious and methodologically consistent way. The research produced by the economists working for international organizations is 75 percent worthless because it's too sloppy and lacks a sound scientific basis.
- Society is willing to pay for their services.
- Economists have a big role in that they have managed to make their discipline inaccessible to other social scientists, or to non-economically-educated people. Therefore they can claim everything they want and just pretend that it is right because "that's what economics says." Obviously by "economics" they mean mainstream neoclassical economics.
- In discussion, people use the concepts and the numbers the economists develop.
- I'm not sure we are able to translate our knowledge into real-life answers to

real-life questions. It is my belief that this is not due to the fact that our knowledge is useless. Begs a statement of what it *is* due to.

- There are economists who have an (important) impact on society and help the taking of better decisions either through their research or by doing policy or other advice.
- Economists are colonizing a wide range of disciplines, from history to politics. They try to understand the deep roots of problems, applying scientific tools and rigorous analysis techniques.
- My answer is only relevant to economists in academia, that is, they do their best for some scientific discoveries. But it is usually the case that they cannot communicate with the rest of the society.
- In areas like central banking, economists do have an influence [for example, Milton Friedman and the idea of the NAIRU (Non-accelerating Inflation Rate of Unemployment)]. When it comes to communicating to the man on the street, I think that, except in rare exceptions (like Paul Krugman), we have a very limited influence.
- First, the tradeoff (between coherence with economics and the political feasibility) politicians apparently face when designing policies seems to me an obstacle to making economics more relevant. Second, a huge part of economics, even though interesting, has actually very little relevance to society.
- Economists, though often thought of as being cold-hearted, approach all problems with a rigorous logic that helps to put (social) problems in a context that makes finding solutions a bit easier.
- Many fields in economics have provided very relevant ideas for socioeconomic policy, with practical results.
- They mostly have a role in providing information, either for public opinion of for administrations. I don't like it when they tend to go into sociological debates to extend their cynical reasoning to fields where money is not the main issue. In that case, they are most likely to miss the key points by focusing on "monetizing" things that are in any way difficult to value.
- First, policy-makers listen to economists' opinions more than to any other academic discipline so they are de facto important. Second, the tools of economics are very useful for understanding important economic aspects of society. However, I would qualify this by saying that far too often economists get lost in their models and fail to understand where they do and do not apply, at times applying them blindly and indiscriminately.
- What Keynes said about economists and academic scribblers is still true— perhaps now, however, the difference is that there is a lot more scope to make a difference as an economist in one's own lifetime.
- [Quoting]: "Hyperbolic discounting never pushed anybody above the poverty line." But: I think economists do have a better clue (than politicians for instance) on how to deal with things such as economic policy: auctions applied to property rights for instance; finance, and so on. The thing is that most of the time we do the "dirty job" in the shade and nobody notices it, but that is ok.
- I think economists have a good approach to understanding human behavior and they can contribute significantly to policy formation.
- Government needs advice.
- In some areas where economists are needed and a little bit of economic analysis can generate huge social gains, there is no economist present. On the other hand, many economists and a lot of economic studies are market driven. It

could be beneficial, though. Many economists seem to be blind as to what they are doing.

- Everything is about economics!
- In Germany, public knowledge about economics is so bad that it is difficult for "proper" economists to be heard among the many distorting voices of politicians, union leaders, and "alternative" economists.
- Economists help to solve the problems of society, proposing the concepts and analyzing actual policies. Even though it is hard to persuade politicians to implement the solutions of economists, I think economics works.
- Economics itself is certainly relevant; however, I have some doubts about the quantity of research which sometimes I consider to be too great (relative to its cost).
- Economists are often unable to cope with real-world problems because they do not consider aspects that are not captured by economic models. Still, they have political influence.
- At least in Germany, neither the public debate nor actual political decisions seem to be much influenced by what economists think about things.
- I actually think that economists are the real politicians today. As unemployment and poverty become more and more important as political topics, economists get more and more influence as they are regarded as specialists for economics-related topics.
- Today the economists could change the world, but economics is always led by political points of view, so they are relegated to marginal roles in the decision process. Moreover, between researches, the economists are considered less important for their particular role.
- Policy-makers increasingly rely on economists—a good reason to have some decent answers.
- People tend to believe them. Hence, they are relevant since they can affect expectations and guide policy choices. Actually, they know very little and in practice can do even less.
- Economists are reasonable people and are able to form reasonable positions on many points. You see this reflected in the fact that in most governments a lot of positions are taken by economists.
- I do not think that economists play a determinant role in political decisions, except when they do not act as economists, but as politicians (at least in Italy)!
- Economists can affect the general feeling about an economic issue, but this takes time—and luck!
- A lot of research is meaningless for thinking about and acting on real-world problems.
- The more our future is depending upon our expectations, the more the role for magic is increased.
- I consider that economists have helped to address relevant questions in policy matters, such as monetary policy, among other relevant questions for human welfare in general.
- Economic issues matter a lot for people. Hence economists are important.
- If economists have something relevant to say, they are listened to. But nobody outside the profession cares too much about the irrelevant or very non-robust results that economists often produce.
- I think we have a value in society but I think economics has, to some extent, lost its direction. I have been to a lot of seminars where people have very elegant

mathematical models, and they have a beautiful proof, but they have no idea of how the parameters relate to "reality." This inability diminishes our potential role in society.

- I do not know what is really going on in the world yet.
- For the most part, economists cannot give explanations. For example, recently a friend asked me to analyze the balance sheet of the firm he's currently working for and to give him some advice regarding his permanence in this firm. My answer: "I don't know." He probably wonders whether I actually know anything relevant at all!!!!
- Because most things economists do are completely irrelevant to the real world. And if some things are relevant, economists cannot communicate the relevancy.
- Politicians still believe in traditional Keynesian policy and most of the discussion focuses on these kinds of policy intervention.
- Look at issues in ways that are different from other approaches.
- Economists have no clear opinion, therefore the role they play in society is not very present; also the social status is low. On the other side, advising governments and institutions, they have a strong influence on the economic policy and therefore on the society.
- The few economists that do venture off in the public policy debate seem to have an enormous impact. Their opinions are often not even questioned.
- Economists shape policy, and their models seek to explain and predict social phenomena.
- Economic problems are increasing and affect nearly everybody. Economists try to give help to politicians.
- Their comments, remarks, and opinions are viewed as relevant by the general public, but someone who goes through the training starts doubting that relevance seriously.
- There exist many problems in our current society that can be studied in economic terms, such as unemployment, optimal taxation, environmental issues, or even marriage.
- People take economists' opinion into account, but there is no real analysis of their arguments.
- Most of them seem to be pure theorists and their first best solutions are often politically not feasible; that is, the general public and politicians think that "What you propose may be nice and clever, but, sorry, it is not feasible."
- Too abstract. Also, I am not sure if academic economics should have any policy relevance. Consultancy work might have some relevance.
- The main mistake economists make is to build castles in the sky. Economists should lobby hard to get economics to school. That is, economics should be taught at the same time as physics and chemistry and the average person needs to know and understand much more about basic economics.
- The link between economics as a science and the political decision process is very weak; there is little communication and exchange of ideas.
- There are relevant and useful things economists can do; on the other hand, they are more ideological than they would like to admit, which may lead them to harmful advice (Friedman seems one like that).
- It seems that results presented by economists are used to promote policies, opinions, and so on, but only in cases where the results fit the aims of policy-makers. Many results are overlooked.

- Economists in the academic area sometimes seem to be too far from real-world economic concerns.
- There is a wide gap between theory and actual practice.
- Germany is mainly ruled by lawyers—economists have less influence. This situation might change soon.
- In the positive sense, their relevance is for satisfying scientific curiosity, in this case about human behavior. In the normative sense, their relevance is in providing centered, scientifically-based policy recommendations (as good as possible).
- We included in the mainstream of economics several new things: the role of information, institutions, dynamic aspects of economics, and so on. One example in macro: fifty years ago we didn't know exactly how monetary policy works in an open economy with dollarization. Now, I suppose we have some idea about that.
- Because sometimes economists find it hard to talk about what people really need.
- On practical grounds, the great majority of economists end up recommending policy based on their common sense and expertise rather than their real economic knowledge. Politicians also listen to economists on the basis of their common sense, while the business world is an issue of power. So scientific knowledge in economics is widely ignored.
- Economists are considered important because the economy is important in the daily life of everyone. (Most of the people, however, ignore the difference between economy and economics.)
- If the question means whether any economist has a relevant role in society, Yes, for sure. I don't know whether those economists are the best among their colleagues.
- Economics is important (although not unique) in determining rules and making decisions.
- Maybe the "theory of politician game" is more important.
- Just read a book named *Freakonomics: A Rogue Economist Explores the Hidden Side of Everything* [Levitt and Dubner, 2005] where the authors had explained the economics related to all our daily stuff. That's why I decided to get a graduate education in economics: to understand the world, or our society.
- They are very much respected, which gives them a voice in all the problems of society.
- We are responsible for providing politicians and public opinion with sound information on feasibility and effect of policy in many fields (environment, health, education, pensions, and of course monetary policy, trade, and so on).
- Economic analysis is one of the backgrounds political decisions are taken against.
- They govern many important decisions in government and business.
- But less than they think. They are reformed or a kind of "guru." Economics has become a leading discipline and market economy is the only ideology.
- Because they are mainly focused on their own research.
- A critical role in people's well-being.
- Very limited contribution in understanding systems economically.
- When referring to economists, in Italy people say, "You don't want to work?!"
- In my field: OECD, European Commission, open to ideas in general, economists have debates (not academic, but trained in looking at adjustments and journalism).

- I think economics is often used to justify, ex post, decisions that have already been taken.
- Economic thinking is becoming the relevant position.
- They can address policy issues concerned with economic situations.
- Economists can influence policy-makers to avoid the most fatal errors.
- Yes, but society does not always distinguish the difference between economists and businessmen.
- I cannot find any reason why "Yes."
- They do not participate enough in the public debate.
- They define the allocation and distribution of resources.
- Findings and advice from economists are most of the time tweaked to fit political interests, making the economist a convenient scapegoat for unpopular or pork-barrel politics. I took a guess at "tweaked." Maybe you have a more informed suggestion.
- But I think with academics, in each exposure in the media, too little guidance is given for policy-makers.
- I believe it is good: for instance with proper tools to evaluate labor market problems.
- To clean up all the myths and misperceptions that exist on how a market-economy works.
- Newspapers are filled with economists' opinions.
- A lot of research seems irrelevant for policy, and so on.
- Unclear question. But economists have a lot of influence, so they surely are relevant.
- Relevant but communication skills are way too poor.
- Too much influence over actual policy.
- Economic theories seem to be specific, not allowing for global understanding.
- Economists have influence, so they are relevant, even if their opinions are confused.
- It depends. In France, I don't think that professional economists play a big role in public discussions or public policy.

PART 3

Student interviews

6. LSE interviews

There are two LSE interviews. Each interview is with three male students. The students are from a variety of countries throughout Europe and one student is from North America.

INTERVIEW 1

Do you consider yourselves a representative sample of the students here?
As a group, we're not too bad. None of us are English, which is consistent with the student body. But by subject, we're missing a theoretical econometrician.

We have three men here. Is that representative of the student body here?
In my year there was a 50–50 split.

That's quite unusual. I would think that in the entire PhD program, there are about 25–30 percent women.

In Track 2, there are many more men than women.

Would you think I would get different results if I had women here being interviewed?
I suspect you might, but I have no idea what they would be.

I have seen no gender difference in the type of issues students complain about.

How did you each get into studying economics?
I studied industrial engineering in my home country before I came here, and that was 20 percent pure economics. I found that the issues that were raised were very interesting, and tools that were used to answer questions were interesting. At first, I tried to get into a PhD program in my home country, which at the time seemed like the option to take. But I chose LSE because it was considered more valuable internationally. I have been quite happy here.

I chose economics as an undergrad because I wanted a branch of applied mathematics that wasn't mechanics, engineering, or physics, and I ended up really liking economics when I took it in high school in Ireland. I didn't realize that it was as mathematical as it turned out to be, but I have really enjoyed the mathematical component of it. Then, in my final years, I was focused on the applied work, which is how I ended up working for the government and for a consultancy. Having worked there, I realized that it is best to be as far advanced academically as possible if you want to do applied work. Since I've come back here, I've really enjoyed the more academic side of the field. I don't know where it is going to end up.

I had a good teacher and so I enjoyed economics in school, which led me to do an undergraduate degree in economics. Then, after that, I did an internship with a central bank. I decided to do a post-grad and since I was in London, the natural place to do it seemed to be LSE. I always had in mind that I would do a PhD; I didn't want to be the least educated in my family. I really enjoyed policy work, but I decided to come back to school because there is value in being as qualified as you can be if you are doing policy economics. I also applied to the US, and I got in at a number of places, but none of the offers were so great as to overwhelm the advantage of being in London. So I chose LSE and I haven't regretted it.

It sounds like you are all happy with your education. Would you say that most students are?
Recently there was a survey of the students done. About a third of the students replied, and of those, more than 75 percent were satisfied with their supervision, which is a major component of your education in the PhD program.

There seems to be more a discussion about policy here than I noticed in the US. Would you say that's because of the particular group here, or would it be a characteristic of LSE?
That may be because two of us are studying macro policy.

Where do you see LSE ranking in the world? Give me a number 1–100?
Twelfth.

Inside the top ten.

Eight to 12, but it has gone up in the last year since I've been here. [General laughter] Correlation, not causation.

How does LSE's education differ from the top ten US schools?
I would say it doesn't differ, since they have moved to the two-year course

work, two-year research model. In terms of European departments, that was revolutionary.

I don't know. They all seem to offer the same type of thing. In general, I'd say it's very similar.

I would say that the options are less narrowly defined. You can go deeper into specific issues in the US than you can here. But I've only compared it to a few very good US universities.

What is the background of most students? How many students come
directly from university, and how many work before?
More have worked.

The program is now in the process of transition, and a lot of people get a Masters at LSE, then work, and then come back for a PhD. You come back into the MRes (Master of Research), but you've already got the MSc (Master of Science). Certainly, in my year, most people were undergrads who came straight in, or who had taken a Masters program in-between.

When we started the MSc, I would say that only a few people had worked between the Bachelor and the MSc. Even the British, who have more of a tendency to get experience in jobs than, for example, Germans, came directly from university in my year, and then decided after the MSc to do some work.

Would you characterize the training here as preparing you to become an
academic, or to go into applied policy?
My experience with the macro people is that there is a push toward academics. They really want you to churn out a good academic job market paper, and go on the job market and make LSE look good. That's not to say that if you didn't make the top grade academically, that you are not going to be good enough for policy. But I think that most advisors' assumption is that we want to go into academia.

That certainly is the case with econometrics. They are very focused on pushing you toward academia.

I would say that that is also true for micro.

Earlier, I had the impression that most of you weren't going to follow an
academic route, so are you, and students in general, happy with that focus?
I am planning to follow an academic route.

I wasn't before I came here, but now I also plan to follow an academic route.

The same with me; I'm now planning to become an academic.

What are your prospects? What do you see your job market horizon? What would be a top placement, an ok placement, and an "I really didn't make it" placement?
My preferences are slightly warped, since I don't want to move to the US. I'm only considering schools here in Europe. So for me, teaching at Oxford or Cambridge would be a top placement.

You said Europe, but then you said Oxford or Cambridge. Where do continental schools fit?
Yes, there are schools outside of England, which would be top placements—for example Toulouse in France, or Trinity in Ireland, Tilburg in the Netherlands, and Bocconi in Italy are all very good.

I am prepared to go to the US but in that case, it would have to be a good place.

If you got an offer from a 10–20 school in the US vs. an offer from Tilburg or Toulouse, which would you choose?
Then it would depend on specifics of the university.

I'd definitely choose the European.

I'd almost definitely choose the American, not because I especially want to go to America, but I think for academic careers in Europe, some time in the US is highly valued, even if it is just two years. LSE gets lots of placements—some in the top 20, and more in the 20–40 range. I would take one of those even if it was on my mind just for two or three years, because it will show that I've been integrated into the US market. Then I'd get a ticket to Trinity in Ireland, and do nothing for the rest of my life.

[Laughter]

What do you mean "do nothing for the rest of your life"?
It's a bit of a joke among us. There are lots of good economists in Ireland, but it is a very small industry—it's more a cottage industry relative even to the UK academic community. There are a lot of academics in Ireland, largely former students, who go in and settle down. Ireland is a small country, and it's a smaller environment, and actually, if you want to get into the link between academia and policy, it would be easier to do in Ireland. That's what people do there, because by the very fact of being in the university, you are going to know the policy-makers.

One of the big differences I've seen, and one of the reasons I'm interested in studying European economics, is that there seems to be a much closer connection between academia and policy in Europe than there has been in America. Any connection with messy real-world policy would pull you away from writing papers. In Europe, writing papers was just one part of an economist's output; another important aspect was gaining influence within the policy sphere. That seems to be changing as European schools are following the US model. Any reaction to that change?

If you take the German case, from my perspective, I agree that up to now the focus was less on academia, but then the relevance of the work that was done in academia with the purpose of doing it for policy, from my opinion, there was less relevance of this work to the politicians than is the case here in the UK or in the US. In the US and UK, academics have been much more pragmatic than they have been in Germany.

Do you mean at the top end? That wasn't my perception of what was going on in the US at all.

I've always had the view that certainly in macro, that a good academic has to be very much in touch with the policy, because you have to know what the issues are to write something interesting. But then the top policy guys in Europe are often academics. Consider the Bank of England—Mervin King (Governor of the Bank of England) was a former professor and head of the department at LSE.

In macro, in the US very few of the US students were doing a specialty in macro at the top schools. Because most of what they studied was the DSGE model; they had almost no discussion of monetary or fiscal policy in their core courses, they don't do a lot of time series econometrics, so if none of that fits, it's hard to know where the applied work fits in. It sounds like it is quite different here, especially in macro.

It's always hard because once you go into policy you typically use IS/LM and AS/AD and all this DSGE [Dynamic Stochastic General Equilibrium] stuff is superfluous. I think, however, that the link to policy comes from looking at a real-world issue. If you take the grid of potential models and assumptions and you look for one of these coordinates that haven't been filled in, you have a really easy way to write a model. But whether anyone cares, or whether it is interesting, relevant, or important, depends on your ability to motivate that by something real. I think that's the big link that we generally see in our macro seminars with policy. Very rarely would I see a macro paper being written as a pure policy paper. Usually, it would start out with a real-world problem, and end with a policy recommendation that follows from the model. But in the middle there is all the technical wizardry of DSGE.

Yes, for example, just a couple of weeks ago we had a seminar where someone was presenting a DSGE model and we had a couple of economists from the bank who were actually sitting in. So they view it as being as much in touch with their policy end of things, and they are pure policy. And yet they are sitting there in a pure macro seminar.

It sounds like the connection with the Bank of England and the macro taught at LSE is closer than it is at many schools in the US.
It could be very specific to LSE. LSE is in the heart of London. You can literally get on a bus and in ten minutes, you can be at the Bank of England. There is enormous switching back and forth between senior-level staff at the bank and LSE.

I also think it happens on the fiscal side as well. I can think of some professors who have strong links with the Treasury.

When you come in, can you tell who the stars are going to be?
You can take a guess, but I haven't seen whether my guesses are right yet. If you ask me in five years' time, I will tell you my forecast errors. But I think it is inevitable that you look at people and see some as likely to do well.

I think the difficulty is that you are doing these core micro, macro, and econometrics courses, and everyone is going to go into a really precise area, which might require different skills.

There is also a distinction between research and courses.

But you can tell the people who really easily master the intuition and logic of all the courses, and I think you can extrapolate from that who will likely be good. But someone could be really good in macro, and not so good in micro.

Maybe some candidates really stand out, but I think it is hard to predict. There are so many different things that come into play.

How much training do you get in economic history or history of economic thought?
LSE has an economic history department that is separate from the department.

In undergrad you can get some history, but nobody takes it.

Would you be advised against taking it?
No, it's just that people self-select.

There used to be an option in the history of economic thought, but when I did the MSc it wasn't there. I'm not sure whether it has come back in yet or not. But there is a third year course in the history of economic thought.

When you do the field courses here, do you read the literature and debates in the field, or do you focus on recent work?
They build the field courses up from the literature.

I agree.

What's your view of behavioral economics?
I would say that it's an interesting topic, which is a nice extension of micro theory. I think it remains to be seen how relevant it is, but I think it is definitely good to be working in that direction.

Would you say that that's the view of most of the students here?
Maybe at some point, LSE was lagging behind in terms of their new faculty, but I think they have made some new faculty appointments, so there are more people now working on behavioral economics. I think it is introduced more and more into the syllabus of the micro courses.

How about experimental economics?
That is less so, but I think it is coming more and more.

What is your view of sociology? What's the difference between sociology and economics?
Certainly at LSE there is very little link with sociology. They probably think that we look down on them, and because they think we look down on them, they dislike us. There is just no relation at all. I've taken one sociology course in my life as an undergrad, and I have to admit that I didn't like it. It had a lot of ideas, but was not as rigorous as the economics that I was being taught at the time.

I would say that with the development of behavioral economics, where you take social psychology seriously, I think sociology is one of the things that economics is starting to look at. I would say that that's very interesting. Sociology may be lacking some rigorous analysis, but I think the topics that it covers are certainly relevant.

Are the differences I'm hearing here a macro/micro distinction, with micro people seeing sociology as relevant, but macro people not?
It may well be. I have a similar view of political science and government that my colleague has of sociology. I think they do some interesting stuff, and

it is important to macro issues. We can't apply these same models without integrating political issues. So I find that link more interesting than the link to sociology. I think of the representative agent as sociologically normal.

If he is the representative agent, he's got to be sociologically normal. The rest are just tail ends of the distribution that we don't care about.

[Laughter]

I have no experience in behavioral or experimental economics. I care much more about the frontier of statistics.

In statistics, how much training do you get in time series, classical statistics, and Bayesian approaches?
Personally, I felt that the PhD core for econometrics gave a pretty good theory view of everything, but probably less on the pure statistics, and less in the econometrics. I thought, especially given the history of LSE, the courses didn't have as much time series as I would have expected. I was a bit surprised by that. But it is because we now have a group of people here who are good at panel data and they teach the course. So they teach what they specialize in.

That was my experience as well.

The bias is in who teaches the core course. There are some people here doing hard-core time series. But they are not teaching the core. But I intend to take some electives in time series, and this is a great school to do it.

Who grades the core exam?
The syllabus is set by the department, but they do alter it depending on who is teaching it. There is an attempt to cover a bit of everything.

Do most students make it through?
There is some weeding out, but most who come in finish.

I agree; most people make it through.

What if a student fails the core the first time? Do they have to take the course again with someone else?
Resits at LSE require you to wait an entire year. You have the option of resitting the same syllabus you took, or the next year's syllabus retaking the course.

Two results I found in the survey were that students here in Europe were slightly more liberal than in the US starting out, and that both US and

European students move to the right as they progress in their economics education. Do these results sound correct?
That's consistent with my view of others, but it doesn't fit me.

I think it is certainly true in my case.

But it may not be a special feature of economists; I think it is everyone.

There's the old saying—if you're not a socialist at the age of 20 you've got no heart, and if you're not a capitalist by the age of 40, you've got no head.

[Laughter]

I think that in terms of government objectives, I'm still very liberal. If anything I've gone a bit more to the left. But in terms of the way of achieving those objectives I'm a bit more realistic. I think economics teaches you that incentivization and the right use of market-based policy is the way to go. I'm righter in means, and lefter in objectives.

I agree.

I would also agree. I would be more confident now about the tools to reach a certain end.

In the survey LSE's results differed from the other European school's results in that there was a lot more stress here about course work and finding dissertation topics. LSE's results were much more similar to US school results than were the other top European schools. Any reaction?
I think it is probably because of the two-year core course structure, which is like the US. For example, at a school like Oxford, you are guided into the research, because you have no rigorous training. Here, after you've taken the core courses, your supervisor says "You're at or near the frontier now—show me that you can stay there." You are left to yourself to do it. That would be my guess of why the results differ.

It might have to do with the restructuring. Some people are not very happy in Track 2 where you have course work at LSE that is quite demanding. You have to do dissertations in both years of the Masters as you go along. That may have caused some stress for a subgroup of students.

Any final comments?
I think it would have been very interesting if you had done this survey at LSE ten years ago. I think LSE is still in the middle of a huge transition period, having been one of the top programs in the world. It really fell off

its perch in the mid-1990s, and went through a lot of problems. But thanks to a lot of hard work by the department over the years, it has rebuilt itself very well. Various specialties are moving from "good and strong" to "very strong" now. I'm certainly very happy with it.

I agree.

INTERVIEW 2

How did you get to LSE?
I did math and computational neuroscience as an undergrad. I ended up in economics because it is a field that allows you to ask interesting questions. I like that it is more precise. I decided to come here because I was in London already. I didn't seriously consider other universities.

I did my undergrad in Scandinavia in physics, math, and statistics. I came into economics because I liked the scientific method, but I was more interested in the problems of society than the problems of natural science and engineering. If you are interested in the problems of society, and you want to use mathematics and statistics, there are not many fields you can go into. That's why I'm in economics. I had done a Masters here, so I was here already, so I decided to stay. I applied to the US and UK, and chose the UK because it is closer to home.

I am not English, but I did my undergrad in England. I did physics for four years as an undergraduate, but I was always interested in social-science-related problems. I specifically got interested in understanding what trade and globalization were doing to the world, and I kept being frustrated by the things I read. I thought that there had to be scientific answers to these difficult social questions, just like the kinds I'm used to reading in physics. So I decided to try studying economics seriously.

Do you consider yourselves representative of the student body?
We all seem to have studied math and physics before we came here. I'm sure that we're not the only ones, but I don't think that's the case for everyone.

Probably you would find more students who went straight from school to graduate work in a matched sample, although the number is probably less than in the US.

I don't know many North Americans, so I'm not representative.

The lack of a native British student here is representative of LSE.

How about the lack of women? Would women's views differ from yours?
There are some women, so we're definitively not a matched sample in that dimension, but I can't think of any views that would be significantly different, although it depends on what you ask.

Are you happy with your education here?
I'm happy with the PhD program. I wasn't so happy with the Masters program, which I took under the old system. It was a year in which I learned a lot based on my own readings and it was a good year socially. But the quality of the education was not strong. The PhD program has been much better. I have a strong impression that supervision is less active over here than it is in the US. You are left to your own devices a lot more, at least from the stories I've heard. I heard that over in the US a student got an e-mail from his supervisor that he hadn't seen him in two weeks, and wondered what was up. That wouldn't happen here.

I had a good Masters program here. I thought I was taught quite well. Since my first degree was in physics, they made me do a one-year diploma, which is a one-year undergrad crash course in economics. Then I did a one-year Masters, and moved into the PhD program. In the PhD, I get the impression that supervision isn't quite as hands-on. But it is a nice research group. There are two research centers here—something like the NBER [National Bureau of Economic Research] and there are about 15 PhD students and four faculty who are active in these. That creates a good culture. I feel I've learned a lot in the group, possibly more than anywhere else.

I would agree that the seminars are good. There are lots of seminars. How good the supervision is depends on the supervisor to a great extent, and also on your personality. The courses are not all that great here. I have two problems with them. First, there is a lot of overlap of the Masters with the new PhD; they don't fit together very well. Also, there is a lack of time in the courses, especially in the micro. Another general point, which may or may not be true of other places, there is very little said about the philosophical issues in economics, which are much more problematic than those in physics are. Related to that, there is not a good discussion of the relationship between theory and the real world. There are lots of things in economics that are based on relatively arbitrary assumptions, and they often forget why they made them in the first place. They come to believe that that's how the world is, even though there is no shred of evidence. For example, when exponential discounting was first suggested, I think it was Samuelson who said that this is clearly not realistic in any way. The world is clearly different from this. For example, we may put more weight on the first period, but let's assume for simplicity that this works. A lot of economists forget that the assumption was made for simplicity, and just assume that that's how the world is.

Do you think LSE is different from other schools in this regard?
I have no idea if LSE is different, but I think it would have been better if there was more discussion of the relationship between theories and the real world. There are reasons to assume simple models; they help you think. You can't just make things super complicated, but you should know what you are doing, and why you are doing it.

I agree with that; I just happen to think that it is a problem of economics, not of LSE.

That may well be the case.

Some universities seem to have this mandatory part of the first or second year PhD program in which you have to do an introduction to philosophy.

What schools would have that?
I've seen this course at Harvard. It's called something like critical analysis of economics, which my friends told me was mandatory in the first year. Maybe it was ungraded, but I think you had to attend. [Editor's comment: Harvard does not have such a mandatory course at the graduate level. It has a course at the undergraduate level about which there was some dispute as to whether it could be taken instead of the standard principles course.] That sounds to me like a good idea.

You know that the LSE has some of the best philosophy and history of economics in the world.

Exactly, so it seems a natural place to do it.

You can take advantage of that if you want to, but you certainly aren't encouraged to do so.

They are in different departments and there is little collaboration among departments.

Would all of you see that as a problem of economics?
I very much agree with the general point about the assumptions.

I have two points. I agree that the lack of consideration of assumptions is a problem. In my field, I would love it if the first courses I took had defended the embedded assumption of competitive firm behavior with evidence, or told us that that discussion has never taken place. Second, the discussion about whether it is useful or not—what are the costs and benefits of making these assumptions—in these kinds of models, which is a philosophy of economics or methodology question—that discussion also never took place. It is interesting that there is a free market in which courses we can take here. So we could take courses that question those assumptions, but we don't. So if you believe we are rational, it must reflect that we aren't interested in the question.

If you feel such courses are important, why don't you take them?
I feel it wouldn't be privately rewarded. I think it might be socially optimal, but it would not be privately optimal.

I actually go to some courses that touch on these issues, and the research I'm doing in behavioral economics also touches on them. But on the whole, I think the academic quality in general, rather than specifically something to do with the LSE, rewards specialization. It does not reward broad horizons. I think that is true in general. A stronger statement of this point is that the economics profession rewards a certain kind of professional work over working on important problems.

In one of the interviews that I did in the US, the students made the following joke. Sociologists look at important problems that they can't answer. Economists look at unimportant problems that they can answer. Is that a fair differentiation?
My favorite view of the two is that we study the same thing, but that the methodology is different. I have a hard time delimiting economics from the other social sciences. I think of myself as a social scientist. I just happen to use a certain methodology, which is favored in the economics branch of social science.

And what is that methodology?
It is a more mathematical, empirical approach.

I think a lot of the motivation behind the research in economics is that we find motivation by attacking important problems. I agree that a lot of what is published might be considered by an outside observer as a less important problem. For example, there's growth, there's development, there's an entire normative branch of economics that is tackling important problems. I agree that there is a tradeoff because big important problems are hard to do well, but I don't know whether I would agree with that quote about sociology and economics.

I would disagree with it too. I think growth is an excellent example of an important problem. Actually the practical papers that are written are not always so informative, because it is so difficult to do. But people write papers anyway.

So maybe they end up going down this road and solving unimportant problems within important areas, or at least problems that an outside observer would say are unimportant.

It sounds like you are doing behavioral economics. Is that the micro type that is taught here?
There are not many economists here who do behavioral economics. I was actually at the summer school in a program that focused on these issues, and there are several more students who are interested. There are two young faculty members who are doing behavioral work. But it's not as strong as it would be at Berkeley or Harvard, for example.

One of the things that came out from the interviews in the US was that there was a general feeling that the students are being trained as efficient article writers. I'm getting a different sense here—that it's really answering important questions that is important for you. Journal article writing is not so important. Would that be a correct sense?
That's not what I meant. I think I just meant that the journal editor's objective function has some component of the importance of the topic in it. So behavior that caters to that objective function gives one a push toward looking at important topics.

So the push for working on important issues comes from the journal editors? In the US, my sense was that the view of the journal editor's objective function was that it was relatively narrow—concerned about smaller debates which were amenable to economists' methods, and not toward broader issues about the importance of topics—that the entire process was somewhat of a game. In one interview we had a discussion about what percentage of the articles in top journals might be considered junk. If I were to ask you that question, what percentage of the articles in the top ten journals qualify as junk, what percentage would you give?

[Long silence]

I don't know about junk, but I would agree that a lot of them are not very relevant to reality; they are more like virtuoso exercises that show skill but don't really shed light on problems. In that sense I'd agree with that characterization of junk.

I think it is possible that at the LSE and in Europe that people are not quite as simple as that. There are people who think they are tackling important questions, and I don't think you can go so far as to characterize all the work as junk. I think that it is definitely the case that a lot of people are writing uninteresting papers, and maybe there should be fewer people doing this job around the world.

Where do you see the LSE economics department ranking in the world ranking of departments?
Fifteenth.

Maybe a bit higher than that.

You sound as if you are somewhat familiar with graduate education in the US. How would you say graduate education here at LSE differs from that in the US and at other European schools?
My impression is that people work more in the US than they do here—both faculty and students.

I get the impression that there is a bit more ambition in the US—that there is a very clear game—getting a good job, and that your supervisor is very explicitly teaching you and giving you exercises that show you how to play that game, grooming you—for example, when people are visiting the department, making sure that you as the grad student go to meet them, seeing that you attend conferences. One might say that there you learn hard strategic behavior whereas here we learn more soft strategic behavior of writing good papers and letting the rest take care of itself.

I would agree.

Why do you think there is this difference?
My pet theory is that it is a revealed preference—that there are a lot of people at the LSE who made a choice for non-career-based reasons to be here, and that reveals a taste for non-career ambitions. People have self-selected. I think that there are a lot of people here whose career objective is to get a job at a nice town in their home country in continental Europe and contribute to the local debate there, as opposed to focusing on writing articles and entering the worldwide job market and taking the best job no matter where it is.

I don't know if it is true, but sometimes I think that the US schools are leading a trend, and Europe is just following. It is seeing graduate education as much more of a job training and getting the best possible job rather than deepening your understanding of economic phenomena.

I think there is a broader difference between the US and Europe, and it is not something specific to economics. But I would say that there is overspecialization in academia in general and that overspecialization makes it more difficult for people who are so specialized to make certain types of important contributions to the profession. In that sense, it may actually be that the more European style of education is a better preparation for people to think a little bit outside the box, and make more fundamental contributions to the profession, even though maybe on average the American education would produce better results. This is obviously highly speculative, and obviously, if the best students go to Harvard, that will have its own effect. But I'm not sure that this specialization is necessarily a good thing.

One of the results of the US survey and interviews was that students really felt that they were being trained to write a good job market paper. They distinguished a good job market paper from a good paper. I don't detect that same sense here. There's more focus on just doing good work.
I've encountered the distinction from some faculty members here who were trained in the US, but it is not from the majority of faculty.

In the core courses, what do they teach you, and how does it change from year to year. And how are the exams graded?
It's been a few years. The main book for econometrics was Bill Greene, I think.

For micro it is Mas-Colell, and for macro it changes over time. Macro is the least defined field. Now it is Sala-i-Martin in the first term. Then, in the second term, it is really all over the place, because the person teaching it teaches his own work rather than using a book.

Macro was the same when I took it; they primarily taught their own work. There is a canonical growth text—Sala-i-Martin and Barro. We covered loosely what could be called Lucas-Sargent models but the course was not tightly tied to that.

Would you learn DSGE models? The new Woodford work, for example?
A little bit, but not much.

How important are problem sets in the core courses?
They are graded during the year, but the grades don't count. The only grades that count are the grades on the final exam.

Are the problem sets good predictors of what will be on the final? In the US some of the students referred to finals as "problem-set lite," by which they meant that the problem sets would be good predictors of what the finals would be—probably easier because you'd be limited because you won't have

that much time. You could pass, possibly without really understanding what was going on.
I think a lot of us study the last few weeks before the exam, and we concentrate on old exams.

In the exams the first section is all short answer questions, which are very different from anything you did in the problem sets.

They are more about discussing lecture material, some theorem, or some result, as opposed to solving an explicit problem. For example, the question "What does the literature say about the factor price equalization theorem?" might be one in trade. It is not going through the mechanics.

Is that in the field courses? Trade would have been a field course. Is it also true in the core courses?
Yes, I was just using trade as an example.

Would you cover IS/LM in macro?
My year we didn't, but I was in the newer system.

IS/LM is not in the new PhD course, but it was discussed in the MSc course. It is something that you are assumed to know.

In the field courses, how much reading in the literature would you do?
The field courses are still a bit funny because the MSc program goes parallel to the PhD program, but to save money the two are the same with the PhD students doing an extra module. So if you are a trade PhD student, 80 percent of the trade course is actually a Masters-level field course. They don't have the focus on cutting-edge research. They are very much about the literature as it stood five to ten years ago, and its historical origins. It definitely wasn't an intellectual history approach though.

I have the impression that in the extra unit, they try to bring you up to the cutting edge.

My experience was different. In my field courses we focused on the most recent papers, including working papers in the field courses. There was little about the history of the field, just as there is nothing about the philosophy of the field. Certainly the micro theory courses cover primarily very recent work. That's also true for labor.

One of the general results that come out of the survey was that US students seemed more interested in applied micro, whereas European students showed more interest in econometrics. Any reaction?

Applied micro is a phrase that I hear in the US, but it's not a phrase you hear in Europe.

Modern applied micro includes fields like labor and public finance. It typically includes heavy emphasis on econometric studies and data analysis using generally plausible assumptions—what might be called loose modeling. The work that Steve Levitt does falls within that approach.
There are very few students doing pure econometric theory here.

What would students do here?
A large percentage do development or labor. Others do political economy, labor, trade, macro, and contract theory. That's what comes to mind off the top of my head.

What does political economy include?
It involves including political variables in the analysis—for example, whether democracy matters.

Another result of the survey was that Europeans were slightly more liberal than US students, but that over time, they both became less liberal. Is that consistent with your view?
By liberal you mean left in the American sense, right? That often confuses us. I would agree that there's a movement to the right. That's certainly the case with me.

In the behavioral economics summer school, almost all the faculty were to the left of the political spectrum. Maybe it says something about behavioral economics, and not about Europe.

The new paternalism.

It doesn't fit into the standard definitions because you wouldn't find many people in economics who would endorse a type of anti-globalization left view of policy.

I'm not sure that you would find a lot of people who would endorse the libertarian view either. Most people would say that there's some scope for government action.

At LSE there was more stress about course work and finding a dissertation than there was at other European schools. Any thoughts or reactions?
In the old system there was no required course work. In the newer program there is, and that could induce stress.

It is that LSE is more closely American.

The faculty here keep a close eye on American schools, probably more than on other European schools.

In terms of the PhD program, the economics department within the LSE is a real outlier from other LSE PhD programs. Most of the other programs are this very classic British PhD doing a three-year book-length contribution to the world. At most departments at LSE that is still the model. The economics department differs from the other programs in that students take more than three years, course work is a big part of the PhD program, and generally economic dissertations involve three essays, rather than a book-length dissertation. LSE is now structured very similar to the US system.

What type of jobs are most students getting?
Most are academic.

What if someone said I really want to go into policy? If they wrote that in their application, would they get accepted, and if you told that to your advisor, would you get less help?
That would not be a problem here. Faculty are definitely doing policy-oriented work. It's not quite policy, but it is very applied—analyzing the results of particular policies. There are a lot of people who work with government.

Are students' job aspirations moving into government or into teaching?
There is moving back and forth.

I don't think that you are strongly discouraged from going into policy. Maybe you would get less attention. I don't see much discrimination.

I think I've seen evidence of an anti-policy bias, but it depends on the supervisor. But another interesting dimension of that would be the decision of whether you would accept a job in the US. I think some faculty would give less emphasis to those students who want to go back to their home country, rather than being willing to accept the highest-ranking job they get offered.

They want to push people to apply to academic positions.

Does that work out for most of the students? What happens to the 20 students going out each year?
There are 20 students going in; the number coming out is slightly less. Of the ones coming out, at least half, and probably two-thirds, go into academia to either a good European school, or a not-so-good American school. Of the ones going on to academia, probably two-thirds go to Europe.

There are also some who go to the private sector, and some go to international organizations such as the IMF.

Any final comments?
On the issue of Europe vs. America, one thing that has come up in student discussion is that economics is a US-biased field, by which we mean that the journals focus on US issues and data. Suppose that you could look at a policy that's been done in Denmark and also in some state or city in the US. The journals' inherent bias will be toward the US policy discussion with US examples.

In terms of papers that you're writing, where would your advisors suggest that you send them?
I'm working on a paper but I haven't thought of journals yet.

I have not sent a paper out yet, but my supervisors would put a strong stress on doing papers that would go in the top five journals or not writing them at all.

I would agree that that's the advice we would get. My advisor has been encouraging me to focus on what will be the job market paper, which he definitely would want to be publishable in a top five journal.

7. Pompeu Fabra interview

Universitat Pompeu Fabra is a relatively new university in Barcelona, Spain. It was established in 1990, and has quickly established a reputation as one of the top universities in continental Europe teaching US-style economics. The interview is with four students—two from Latin America and two from continental Europe. They are in their third through fifth years.

INTERVIEW

How did you happen to come to Pompeu Fabra?
I am from Latin America. I applied to US universities, but then a friend of mine suggested that it is better to try a European university. Since I didn't have much information about schools, I relied on his recommendations. He recommended Pompeu Fabra and Tilburg.

Although I am from continental Europe, I did my undergraduate degree in England and by the time I applied for graduate programs, it was too late to apply to either the US or the UK. So I knew that I would have to go to a school in continental Europe. I asked my professors, and they suggested a number of schools, of which this was one.

I am also from continental Europe. My decision to come to Pompeu Fabra was based on my preference for finding a good economics program in Spain.

I am from Latin America as well. I was studying in Prague, where I did a Masters degree. I wanted to do a PhD at a good university in Europe and Pompeu Fabra was one of them.

Would you see yourself as representative?
We're missing the Italian contingent; there are a number of Italians here.

Actually, the Italians have been decreasing in the last couple of years and are being replaced by a Turkish contingent.

Eastern Europeans also are missing; they have been increasing in numbers as well. But it is true, there are a lot of students here from Latin America.

If you hadn't been accepted here, what would you have done?
I would have gone to another economics program. If I hadn't gotten into any program I would have studied finance or administration and then found a job in my own country.

I probably would have worked for a year and then reapplied here or elsewhere.

I would have finished my earlier studies and then applied to an international organization.

Do most students work before coming here?
Most Latin American students work before coming.

A significant minority of the students have worked.

How do most students finance their education here?
In the second year, everyone gets a grant, which is tuition plus 1000 euros a month for 12 months.

If you know Spanish, there are also jobs as teaching assistants [TA] that many students do.

The program here is described as a pyramid, with the Ms, the Mas and the PhD. Can you describe the path that most students follow?
Even if you have a Masters, you have to do the Masters here again. So you have to do the Masters first. Of all the Masters students about a third of the students take the exams, and about a fourth of the students pass.

Why so few students taking the exam?
They are discouraged.

And many of them decide they don't need it. At least in Europe, the Masters serves students well as a degree to get a job in business.

A Masters isn't necessary to find a good job in business.

It depends on what country. For example, in Germany, the BA doesn't mean much.

Is the Masters from here valuable as a job market credential?
That's certainly our impression.

What do the students who drop out do?
A few go to other similar academic programs.

One of the reasons for that is that the Italians only get funding to go to a program outside of Italy for one year, so they go back to an Italian program.

How many students are there in your typical class?
The whole program has about 100 students with about 60–70 economics students. I would say that almost all of the economics students come with the intention to do a PhD. After one term many decide maybe not here, and maybe never. The finance program and management programs are different, because their Masters degrees have more market value than economics.

With the large number of students dropping out, is there a bad feeling among the students?
I think there are different factors. Some come in and decide that graduate economics is not what they thought it would be based on their undergraduate experience. Then, there are some who think that this isn't the right place for them.

I think the students who find it different from what they expected are not happy. They feel cheated by economics.

There are a lot of complaints about the program among the students. They feel that they don't learn anything useful.

There are some who feel that they haven't been taught well, and others who feel that it is unreasonably hard. And of course there are the financial issues; scholarships here are not as competitive as at some of the other similar schools.

If you come from an undergraduate program, you can find yourself at a competitive disadvantage, competing with students who already have a Masters before they come here, as is the case with many Latin American students.

How are the classes structured?
In micro, it is Mas-Colell almost word by word, starting with Chapter 1 and working through Chapter 6.

Then you have problem sets, but there are solution manuals that you can copy and hand in. Then, the TA puts an OK on it. What matters is whether you hand it in.

Problem sets don't count much for grades in any of the courses.

Actually, here it is never quite clear what determines your final grade. There are cases where doing well on problem sets can help.

Even if they don't count much, the problem sets create a huge pressure among students, and all the students stress about handing them in.

Especially at the beginning when you aren't clear about how things work.

Eventually, networks develop and students work with other students. The networks interrelate, so the answers spread out among most students.

I always got help.

There was a preliminary math course, and after the exam for this course, we got a short speech from the director who told us that it is going to be ridiculously hard, and there a lot of people here who are not suitable for the program, they will have to struggle and work 24/7. From that point on everyone was very scared and was cooperating a lot.

Our speech was slightly different; we were told "Now you will learn how to fail."

He said it in a nice way; I actually got a good impression. He said that maybe before you were at the top of your class, but here, you may not do so well, and decide that this isn't for you. He was kind of comforting.

Maybe we had the same speech, but heard different things.

I think what he wanted to say was that it is going to be tough, but don't be miserable.

Is it tough?
Yes.

Could you describe a typical day for a student in the first year?
In my first year my day normally started at 7:30; I was in the library by 9:00am and I was there essentially until midnight, when I went home, read another hour and went to sleep.

I also got in about 9:00am, then had about two or four hours of lectures. Then, with some breaks in the afternoon, I worked seriously until about 11:00pm or so.

I had my Masters before coming here, and it was a good program. So here we did general equilibrium in two weeks; I had already had a complete course in general equilibrium. So I had it much easier than them. But I did some work.

Grades here are 1 through 10, right? What is passing?
A 5 is passing.

How are the exams for the courses structured?
In general the exams were very closely related to what was covered in the lectures and problem sets, although I'm not sure everyone in my year felt that way. That's quite different than it is at, say, Cambridge, where the exams often cover quite different areas than the lectures or problem sets. Here you knew what was expected. However, it was never quite clear what the standards were. The exams were either too hard or too easy, which meant that everyone thought they failed and discovered they did better than they thought, or the opposite.

The grade distribution here is cooked all the time.

By that do you mean the grades are normed or curved?
Not officially, but they are unofficially.

Essentially, there are three core exams—micro, macro, and econometrics, and there is always one outlier, so they do whatever they want to afterwards. With one outlier exam, they just give the grades randomly. It's the same with the PhD entrance exam, which is definitely harder than the class exams.

Exactly, I fully agree.

Officially, there is supposed to be an objective criteria. Unofficially, the criteria are much more subjective, because they have a capacity limit on the number of students they want to let into the PhD.

In one year, the average in the econometrics was 3.5 so they had to lower the standard.

If students fail, can they take it again?
You can take the PhD entrance exam a second time, but you have to wait a year. Even people from outside can take them.

The entrance requirements are changing and they are still modifying it. We were guinea pigs.

One of the results of the survey was that European students had less stress than US students. I'm not necessarily hearing that from you.
I think they are trying to copy the US system, so I feel that they are trying to add pressure.

The stories we hear about the US are actually that it is worse than it is here. At least from the second year on, once students get into the PhD program, the stress decreases here.

In the US we hear that the stress continues, and they all are working until three or four in the morning. We believe that we also have a life; we still work a lot, but there is a limit.

My theory about this is that from the second year on, it really becomes intensive. So you really need much more assistance. Here they don't give you all that much help, and in exchange, they let you get away with doing less.

I think the first year is quite similar to the US. In the second year, I think it is true that the professor doesn't give you too much support. You have to do it on your own. In the third year, as you approach getting on the job market, you put more pressure on yourself.

I'm not advanced enough to make a judgment. In the second year, you are still taking some courses, which in theory you need to get passing grades, but the grades are higher, so in fact, that is not a serious hurdle.

In the US the second year courses are called field courses. Here, are those field courses also highly mathematical, or are they more literature review classes?
They are highly mathematical.

That I think is another difference between here and the US. Here the second year courses are still quite mathematical, with little or no writing. I think it is a problem.

How many second or third year students are working on an article for publication?
Almost no students in the second year are. We have to do a paper for the class, but we are not thinking about publication.

Perhaps if you were doing some joint work with someone, you might, but it is not the norm.

One of the survey questions concerned monetary and fiscal policy. Where would your answer to that have come from?
In our monetary course, we spent three lectures deriving a theorem, which essentially said that if you print money, there will be inflation. So I should really know that. My feeling is the information we are learning is becoming less and less applicable. You have to show that you are smart. How do you show it? Doing derivatives, or set theoretical proofs.

Exactly.

It depends on who is teaching.

It depends on the context. I remember that I was once in an interview for a summer job, and they asked a macro question. Even though I had in the back of my mind all the real business cycle stuff, the answer I gave was on the basis of IS/LM. It just makes intuitive sense.

I think I wouldn't give any answer, because I have no clue about monetary and fiscal policy.

[Laughter]

I got a good grade in the monetary course, but I got a good grade because I know some math, and I could do the models. But I never understood what monetary policy or theory is about. I didn't know it before and I don't know it now.

I would give the response based on IS/LM and I think policy-makers in the world would also do so.

So you can pass the course without understanding anything about policy?
There are micro foundations for IS/LM so it is fun.

When you come in, can you tell who the stars are going to be?
In terms of the students, no.

There was a correlation between how well people understood the problem sets and how well they did on the prelims.

What do you mean by "best student"? The skills that you need for the first year are different than the skills that you need later on. I did quite well in the first year, and then I didn't do well afterwards.

You need a lot of self-confidence and internal fortitude in later years. You can be a genius and not do well.

Are you happy with the degree of policy discussion that you are getting?
I think most of us would like less math, or at least more intuition.

I think the macro course has changed every year. We all had different teachers. In some years there is more policy discussion—sometimes too much because you are tested on the underlying models, not on policy questions.

Most of the people who want more policy discussion don't stay. You should really talk to the people who have left the program.

A lot of people come here because they had lots of policy discussion when they were an undergrad. They actually love the mathematical stuff initially because they think it has to be important. But then they get tired of it when they figure out that it is not.

Do you get any discussion of methodology?
None.

How would you distinguish mainstream economics from heterodox economics? What does "heterodox" mean?

Non-orthodox. In the US there are feminist economists, Austrian economists, and radical economists, all of whom would be considered heterodox.
Before I came here, I would have said that anything that doesn't involve rational agent maximizing assumptions was heterodox, but now I realize that there are loads of people even here who use other assumptions and publish in mainstream journals.

Every year there are more non-mainstream economists.

That's mainly because mainstream economics cannot explain many issues.

Or has mainstream economics become broader? Heterodox economics is that economics that they would not teach students in a standard program.
There are some topics that are fashionable at the moment that your professor might be working in. They will be the topics that will be discussed.

For example, we have a big group now doing experimental economics, but this is probably already mainstream.

Let me name some economists and see if you are familiar with them. How about Joan Robinson?
Yes, I would know.

No, I'm not good with names.

John Hicks?
Yes.

John Stuart Mill?
Yes.

I can't say I've read him, but I have heard of him.

Hayek?
Yes, but these are all ones we read as undergrads, not in graduate school.

What do you think of Keynesian economics?
I'm doing a monetary economics course now, and I think that in practice, Keynesian economics is something that is important and is underrated by people who pretend that there is not much theoretical validation. I think, however, that most policy-makers work with what is essentially Keynesian economics, which suggests to me that it remains hugely important.

As an undergrad I did IS/LM models, and then as a grad student I did real business cycle models. Personally, I don't fall in either extreme. I don't believe that there is one truth.

In the year and a half that I've been here, the first time I heard the word, involuntary unemployment, is last week. I don't know whether this is a university bias or an economics bias.

Actually, if you were to ask me what is new classical and what is Keynesian, I wouldn't remember.

But I believe that we are specializing in techniques, and there is not much room for other issues. Even the discussions in seminars are on technical issues.

What's the difference between positive and normative economics?
Normative is how it should be, and positive is how it is.

Normative is forbidden.

In the survey, it seemed that US students were more interested in applied micro than European students. Does that fit your sense?
Although I'm doing applied micro, this is a macro school, so it does fit. But there are a lot of people doing applied micro here in Europe.

How would you define applied micro?
I'd say you take empirical facts and try to explain them using a utility maximizing model.

Actually, you don't need to use utility maximizing model. Sometimes, you can just use reduced form equations and that's it.

But utility maximization is implicitly there.

Have you liked the program here?
Yes.

Knowing what you know now, would you have come here?
Yes.

What would you describe as the program's strengths and weaknesses?
The program has a strength in macro; there are some well-known professors, but it is not easy to work with them, because they have limited time.

I found that even during the Masters year that it is relatively easy to get access to faculty, not for long periods of time, but you can create a space, and discuss an idea. One advantage for me is that here there is not much emphasis on knowing theoretical economics. In other places, it is a large part of the core curriculum. But people likely differ in their views on whether this is an advantage or disadvantage.

In applied micro, the strength is that there is a dynamic young faculty. The weakness is a lack of coordination and no way to push the people.

How would Pompeu Fabra rank in terms of Europe and globally?
I would see it second or third in Europe. It depends on fields. In macro, we compare to LSE.

For me it ranks higher, because I wouldn't like to be in the US. It depends.

There are the top schools in the US, then there is LSE, and there are European schools like Pompeu Fabra.

What jobs do students get after graduating?
It is difficult to find a job in the US. Personally, I don't want to go to the US, but I think some students do; it is difficult for them.

I think the people who want American positions are interested in the career aspect of it. They would take an equally good position in Europe if it existed, but it doesn't in terms of reputation. The recent job market experience suggests that graduates can get good academic positions in Europe.

People have gotten offers from the US and rejected them, and have chosen to stay in Europe. Most try to stay in academics, and go into banks and research institutes as a fallback.

I think people here are more open to non-academic positions than they are in the US.

Where do you expect to be in five years or ten years?
I don't know—most likely in a central bank or a big research institute.

I'd like the idea of an academic position partly for itself and partly because it seems to be easier to move from academia to something else than the other way around. It keeps options open.

You got me at a wrong point. I'm thinking about the issue just about every day. I want to be at a university where you can teach. I want to teach.

Does any of your training prepare you to teach?
As a teaching assistant, they give you a high teaching load. We have to teach eight hours a year, which means four courses. I'm TAing in econometrics and labor.

I would like to do economic research.

If you tell your professor that you don't want to go into academia would that reduce their interest in you?
You wouldn't want to say that. The official line is that they are training academics.

You can say that you are doubting, but then they will argue with you that you really like research. They will channel you into a decision where you don't want to be.

I had some friends who when they told their professors that they weren't going into academics, saw a change in their professor's interest.

Where is the job market in Europe?
In the US.

[Laughter]

How do you all expect to find a job?
Most students do the same thing that US students do—they enter the US job market at the AEA. But there is now a Spanish job market, but most people go to the US even to find a European job. Afterwards, there is a British job market. They are now discussing creating a European job market. [Editor's note: the Spanish job market has expanded into the European job market, but it is still in the formative stages.]

A lot of the German academic jobs don't hire through the US job market.
Someone wouldn't go here who wanted such a job. It would be a waste.

For a Latin American, following an academic career means living abroad. There are very few places in Latin America that are reasonable places to aim for. You go there if you don't get an offer in Europe or the US.

Some students that I know chose to go back for personal reasons.

Any final comments?
If you only think you want to do it, don't; you have to really want to do it.

I think there is too much competition. You should know that you will have to do it on your own.

I thought I was coming to do the science of capitalism. I realize now that it is just a business. Some people sell sausages; we sell papers. So this was disappointing to me. But that is personal.

Along those same lines, you will be submitted to a lot of rituals. The strangest aspect of it is that all throughout your schooling, you are being integrated into a community and language. That's the way it happens.

8. Bocconi interviews

There are two Università Bocconi interviews. The first is with four students and the second is with three students. Two of the students are in their second year, three in their fourth year and two in the fifth year. They are a diverse group, and include two Italians, Latin Americans, Western Europeans, Eastern European, and Asian students.

INTERVIEW 1

How did you get here—both in economics and at Bocconi?
I did my Masters in my Eastern European home country. I was thinking of going to the US since as an undergraduate I was an exchange student in the US for a year, and I really liked the style of education. However, when I had to decide I decided I'd prefer to be in Europe than the US.

I was studying in Germany and met a professor who was from Bocconi. He is the reason why I decided to come here.

Bocconi is well known in Italy, so I came here after my undergraduate studies.

After I did a Masters in Latin America, I looked for some good political economics programs. Bocconi was one of those; I applied and got a fellowship here so I decided to go.

How big are the fellowships?
Fellowships are about 600 euros a month. The first year, since you can't teach, it is tough getting by on that, but in the second year it gets a bit better since you are able to teach.

Are you representative of your class?
The student body is widely diverse, and it changes by year. We are probably not representative of the first and second year students, where there are more Italians, a number of whom do not want academic jobs. We are more representative of the students who proceed to their fourth and fifth years.

What's the lingua franca?
Mostly English, especially for the courses, although most of us have also learned Italian. However, we use Italian mostly for communicating with the administration and for our cultural needs, not for our studies.

Did you find learning Italian simultaneously with learning economics in English difficult?
It was actually fun; it wasn't that much of a burden, especially since learning Italian was not compulsory.

What percentage of the students receive financial aid?
Most students get financial aid through the first three years. In the fourth and fifth year there are four scholarships for the PhD. You can also TA.

Some students are accepted without scholarships, and they are allowed to come, but most do not come.

How many students are there in the PhD program?
About 12 to 14 start and about half of them finish.

Can you describe a typical day for students in various years?
The first year is mainly devoted to attending lectures and studying for classes. I'd work about seven to nine hours a day.

The second year still involves some classes, but now there are also seminars which one attends. There are also reading groups. Typically, I'd arrive at the university at noon, and work until 10:00pm.

In the third year, you are working on your research. You are reading papers, books, talking with professors, and writing. You attend seminars. You may also be working as a research assistant or a teaching assistant.

Would you have started writing papers for publication?
Yes, by the time you go on the job market, you should have a job market paper and a paper for publication.

In your fourth and fifth year, you are applying and attending conferences, changing your presentation, TAing, and working on your dissertation.

How much do grades matter?
Grades matter; we have to take two fields, which means that you have to take three courses for each of those fields, plus three additional courses. At the end of the course work, we have to do field exams. You have to have high enough grades to take the field exams. The field exam involves

one section of each of the courses that make up the field. It is essentially a repeat of the courses, and the final grade is given by a committee of the four professors.

What happens if you fail?
Most who fail leave the program, but you are allowed to retake it.

How important are problem sets for grades, and how do students do them?
Sometimes they count for 40 percent or 50 percent of the grade. There were always problem sets. And mostly we worked jointly on them.

One of the results of the survey was that European students were less stressed than students in the US. Is that consistent with your views?
I visited the US and I think it is true. One reason here is that our department is small, and it is easy to know the people around you—both professors and students, and there is also less of a sense of competition among students here.

I don't want to be mean, but in previous years the program was not all that well structured. Now things are changing since we have a new program director. So previously, people didn't have the sense of urgency and deadlines.

Maybe there is a self-selection issue. People who want to relax more come to Europe. Second, most European PhD programs are young programs, and at the beginning there is less stress on the students. The first year students here are really stressed. Many come at 9:00am and stay until midnight, which is when I generally stay until. They are definitely increasing the level of stress.

There is a different philosophy between US and European programs. In the US, it is more paternalistic; the university structure is there to help the students. Here in Europe, it is much more left to you.

What are they training you to be or do?
I'm being trained to do empirical research into political economics.

I'm being trained for an academic career in a university.

I'm being trained to search for new problems that can be solved.

The sense I got from US students was that they were being trained to be efficient journal article writers. Would you say that description fits for you?
That's one of the problems of the program here. They don't teach you to write for a journal. I think that's probably wrong.

They teach us how to do a presentation, but not how to do an article.

I'm doing joint work with my supervisors, and so I am learning by doing.

Not in the program, but I do learn how to write papers in my job as a research assistant.

Are you currently writing a paper that you are thinking of publishing?
Yes.

I should be sending out two papers that I wrote with other students soon.

I've submitted a paper with my supervisor for publication, and I'm working on an extension.

I have written and submitted a paper on my own.

What's the relationship between academic economists and policy?
My field is political economy, so there is a big relationship. We are studying political institutions and using mathematical tools to study the relationship between politics and economics.

It depends on your field. My field is macroeconomics, so fiscal policy and monetary policy are very much something I study.

I do empirical research in public and development economics, so it is quite related.

Do you get any training in methodology, or of how the ideas developed?
It depends on the course.

In many of the courses we are only given the tools, not the context.

That's what you get to some degree in the reading groups. There you see how the methodology matters and how it evolves. These reading groups are especially helpful.

How would you distinguish mainstream economics from heterodox economics? Or would you?
Here we wouldn't. There is no heterodox economics here. We are completely neoclassical here.

Would behavioral economics fall within neoclassical?
Not here.

It is starting here, though. So, yes, behavioral and experimental work can now be considered mainstream.

They gave a course on it here, but most students here don't work on it.

How would you define "heterodox economics"?
Marxist and Post-Keynesian economics would be examples of heterodox economics. I learned about them in my undergraduate work.

In China, I studied Marx; *Capital* is a compulsory course, so I spent a lot of time with that.

You may be surprised, but coming from a former Soviet country, I've never heard about Post-Keynesian or Marxian economics in my studies. However, we did study Hayek and Austrian economics with Western scholars.

If we heard about previous economists or heterodox approaches, it was generally in our undergraduate courses, or possibly in international courses.

In the field courses do you get a lot of training in the literature of your field?
Students get such training more in China than students do here or in the US.

Yes, we get very little of it here.

Is it a problem that they don't teach it here?
I don't see it as a problem; it might be an option.

If I hadn't learned it as an undergraduate, it would be a problem.

I agree.

I don't see it as a problem; I think it would be a different perspective on economics than the perspective of a guy who knows math and solves problems. For publishing articles, I don't think it would be a problem.

But how about for being a good economist—would that matter?
For being a good economist, in the sense that you are able to talk to non-economists, it might be important. But it is not important for the discussion in the field today.

It can help you to have a different way of looking at things and relating more easily with other people.

I think in the Chinese context, it is a matter of being a good intellectual.

I would totally agree. It reduces the need to rediscover things.

Are they not training you here to be a good intellectual?
They are training you more to be an engineer—to solve problems, and do research.

They don't train us in the philosophical aspects of economics.

We don't discuss the main assumptions of the neoclassical model.

Are you happy with the assumptions you are making in the models?
I am.

I think if I am going to be an academic, I should be, at least, self-conscious about these aspects. I would hope that I am sufficiently self-disciplined so that I can read a bit more in the literature, and discuss with some senior professors about such issues.

Do the faculty and student body have any identifiable political persuasion?
No, not that we feel.

We try as economists to be very impartial. The faculty does that very well. Being impartial in an economist's sense is, however, a political view, it is a more classical liberal view.

Do students discuss policy a lot among themselves?
The Italians discuss policy much more than do other students.

That's true.

How would you distinguish normative and positive economics?
I remember the distinction, but I can't do it on the spot.

It is the same with me.

When you study econometrics here, do you focus on times series or cross-sectional work?
We focus on time series.

So would you be comfortable discussing cointegrated vector autoregression?
Yes.

I know a bit about this, but I focus more on micro.

I do macro theory.

What is the theory of macro today?
DSGE models.

Are you comfortable with the assumptions that the DSGE models make? Do you discuss the foundations and assumptions of the model?
I don't feel comfortable with some of the assumptions they impose, but as long as they help you to get results, they can simplify your life and research a lot.

What do you mean "simplify your life"? Are they providing much insight into macroeconomic problems?
Yes, for example, the representative agent assumption is unrealistic, but it helps a lot.

If someone were to argue to you that all the action in macro is in the interaction of agents, which the representative agent model eliminates, how would you respond?
I'd say he's right, but I, nevertheless, am trying to get some implications using a simple toy model, because it is easier to handle and solve.

But if he really pushed you, saying that you have assumed away all the interesting aspects of the model, would you defend the DSGE model, or would you just say, I do what I do?
The DSGE is just our way of doing some part of the research. Maybe in the future it can introduce some other elements. We're looking for micro-economists who can help out in doing this.

How would you respond to someone who said that what you are looking at in political economy is missing many of the dimensions of real-world politics?
You have to close in on certain assumptions and part of reality to be able to study them. Yes, there are many more elements, but initially you have to separate them.

What are the strengths and weaknesses of the program?
I think the strengths are the smallness of the department with very good people in certain areas, so you have access to top professors in certain areas. The weakness is lack of structure, and inappropriate incentives and institutional constraints. For example, to get the research funds here in Italy, you cannot hire students who already have a fellowship. So the professors don't use us as their research assistants.

I think a weakness is that Italy is a highly bureaucratic country that gives us a lot of problems especially for international students.

The degree of liberty, which is both a negative and a positive.

Is the economics profession headed in the right direction?
Yes.

What direction is it headed in? Where will it be in five or ten years?
I think it will increase its consideration of how institutions affect economic issues, and it will incorporate more issues that were not economic. It will also move away from maximizing utility, and become more behavioral.

How does Bocconi rank compared with the other universities in Europe and the world?
The last rank I saw had it at 200 in the world, but I think the department is growing fast, and is a good department, especially on the faculty side.

In Europe I think it is ranked high; it is in the top ten, especially if you exclude the British universities. In the world, it is not so highly ranked, but it is known, and becoming better known; thanks to the faculty.

In certain areas, it is really good.

Are they doing a good job preparing you for the job market?
They help us prepare for interviews; they look at our papers, and allow us to present. They are doing a good job. The problem is not moving us to the paper writing stage in the earlier years, because of incentive problems, such as the fact that research grants in Italy don't encourage it. So we have to do all the early work ourselves, but they are very helpful in the last stage of the job market.

How does the last stage of the job market work?
You present your job market paper here, and they tell you whether you are ready to go or not. They tell us which school we should aim at. They also help us with the costs of sending the applications.

What range of jobs are students coming from here looking for?
I went to the international job market, which is the JOE [Job Openings for Economists] web page and Ionomics. These are US based, but there are European and Latin American schools as well there. But there were few Latin American universities there when I looked. As for the type of job we aim at—we don't aim at the top universities in the US. Moreover, at the lower end of the US market, they still don't know who we are. Another problem of the program here for those who are interested in going into teaching is that you don't have teaching evaluations that you can show even if you are a TA.

What if you told your professors that you were interested in teaching. Would they spend less time with you?
If you were interested in teaching, I don't know why you would be here.

I remember the first time I went to the director of the PhD program, asking whether he could help me become involved in some teaching and research, he completely ignored the teaching and found some research projects for me.

I never thought of teaching here.

Is it because all the undergraduate teaching is in Italian?
No, there are undergrad classes in English.

Where do you expect to be in five or ten years?
I expect to be somewhere in Europe doing applied research.

I expect to be at a policy institution doing research.

I hope to be at a university or research institute, and in five or ten years' time, will also hold a position in China.

I also want to do policy-oriented research, and perhaps work in an international institution, possibly back in my home country.

Are the students generally satisfied here?
All the students complain about the bureaucracy. It takes so much of your time, especially for foreigners. We need a yearly permit to stay, which means you lose time. And you can't travel outside the country without the permit. It takes up to five months to get a permit. Finding an acceptable apartment is difficult; it is expensive, and contracts are in Italian. Opening up a bank account is difficult.

The university doesn't really help, and if there are problems, there is often no one in the administration who speaks English who can help you, which causes problems in the first year until you learn Italian. You are on your own with everything besides your courses.

Would you have come here if you knew everything you know now?
Yes.

Bocconi is part of the EDP consortium, and the Jamboree program they had was useful. I said I was interested in empirical micro, and they told me that I had to go somewhere else. This is an interesting part of the European experience.

INTERVIEW 2

How did you each come to be here?
I rolled into it. After high school I went traveling. When I came back I wanted to do something in an international field and I happened to fall on the brochure of the university that I was going to go to, which was close to where I was living at the time, and they started up a new program in international economics. So I took it and got my Bachelors degree. I was then invited to join a two-year Masters program, and when I finished that, I decided to do my PhD somewhere else. I asked my advisor where I should go, and he suggested Bocconi, which is why I came here.

Did you consider US schools?
No, it was not viable financially.

In my home country, we have a system that after high school you take a college entrance exam, and economics is one of the branches. It was considered one of the best, which is why I chose it. Then I found a job as a research assistant, and I got a Masters in finance. But I didn't like it, so I decided to turn back to my undergraduate field of economics. I chose Bocconi because I wanted to go to Europe and Bocconi was one of the best schools here. I also didn't consider the US, because it was too far and financially too expensive.

After high school, I chose economics by chance. By the end of undergraduate studies, I liked it, and got an offer to study in the US. So I went and got a Masters in the US. Then I realized that I really wanted to do research, and I wanted to come back to Italy, and I chose Bocconi.

How are you financing your education here?
We all have fellowships. But there are also loans since the fellowships are not enough to live on. Some of us also have partners who make money.

Are financial considerations important here?
Yes, Milan is very expensive. I pay more than half of my scholarship for rent.

There are more opportunities to work for Italians than there are for non-Italians.

Could you each describe the typical day, with each of you taking a different year?
That's hard because the program is changing. For the new program, most of the first year students have two classes a day, and the rest of the time is spent on problem sets, reading, studying. They are working all the time.

The new second year involves field courses. Since you choose the fields you like, it is not as hard as first year, and is more enjoyable.

Fourth year students are mainly doing research, trying to complete the dissertation. They also spend part of their time teaching so they can have enough money to live.

Is the change in the program a good one?
It's more like the US program. Whether one considers that better depends.

To be honest, I am not fond of the US program, because I come from a country where the entire PhD program is different. In my home country, you are not a student; you are an employee of the university, and you have four years to complete your dissertation, but there is no course load at all. To be honest, I believe that system works much better, but it does assume that people have a strong background already, including a Masters degree. With the new program, where students start immediately in the PhD program, they often are not ready to make an informed choice, and it is harder for the school to select the appropriate students.

I agree. This new program doesn't make sense for students who already have a Masters degree.

I think it is a good change. It now brings everyone up to closer to the same level to start. That's why the change was made. But the program is relatively young and has been changing year by year.

What is neoclassical economics?
It is the standard approach that economists take.

Is behavioral economics part of mainstream economics?
I would see it as part of neoclassical economics.

How would you define heterodox economics?
A heterodox economist would say that the concept of equilibrium is not the center of economics. They are more interested in dynamics.

Would you be presented with much heterodox economics here?
No, none at all.

Do any of you know anything about Austrian economics?
No idea.

How about post-Keynesian economics?
I heard of it as an undergraduate, but I don't know anything about it.

When you take courses here, do they give you much background in how the ideas evolved, or do they present you with the latest theory?
Mostly, they don't give you any sense of how ideas evolved. They quickly focus in on what is happening right now. They are focusing on the frontier because of the shortness of time.

Are you happy with the way economics is presented here, and are most of the students happy with it?
I would have liked to be exposed much more to the context within which the theory develops, but I am satisfied.

I agree; I'm not happy, but given the constraints, it is reasonable. In every place people complain, and the complaints here are at the normal level.

There are more complaints here, but that's not the university; it is the fact that it is Italy.

[Laughter]

What are the strengths and weaknesses of the program?
I think a weakness is that it is a young program.

That also accounts for some organizational problems. For example, we don't know our requirements. Most of the second year students don't have offices. As for strengths, we have good teachers and Bocconi is well known as one of the best in Europe.

Where does it rank?
It depends on the field. But it ranks high. There are, however, a number of fields that it doesn't have.

What's the difference between economics and sociology?
Math.

[Laughter]

Economics works much more from theory and models, which then uses empirics to test the models. Sociology observes something, and then might try to put a model afterwards.

Sociology has humans at the center; that's not the case for economics.

Do students get a lot of help in the job market?
My supervisors did a lot of work, but the institutional structure is still developing.

How did you prepare for the job market?
At the beginning of September, my supervisor decided that my paper was good enough to go on the job market. Then after that, he explained the nature of the market, explaining how interviews worked. Then in October we had mock interviews. Meanwhile, every student on the job market did a mock presentation of his paper. They also wrote letters of references. Then I went to the US AEA meetings, and interviewed with the European schools. It's really funny. A couple of friends of mine got interviews at schools near us, and they went all the way to Chicago to talk to them. We did get some financial assistance to attend the job market. We also went to the Spanish job market, which is just for Spain. [Editor's note: the Spanish job market has since been expanded to a European job market.] Then in January we went to the English market.

How many schools did you apply to?
Probably about 70. I picked them geographically, because I wanted to stay in Europe. In each country in Europe, there are about three or five universities that hire internationally.

Where do you expect to be in five or ten years?
Outside Italy. No, seriously. I would like to be in the US, not in academia, but I'd like to be working for an international organization such as the World Bank, which means being in the US.

I would like to stay in academia here in Italy, but that is quite difficult even for an Italian. As a foreigner, it is almost impossible. So I will probably be somewhere in Europe. I don't want to be in the US. It is relatively easy to return to my country if one has a PhD from abroad with some type of name.

How would attending Bocconi compare with attending a mid-level US university, say the University of Kansas?
I can't really answer that. I never thought of going to the US. It was too far, and I prefer European culture.

If an Italian wanted to stay in Italy in academia, is Bocconi the best place to go given that the Italian job market is as—shall we say—"institutional oriented" as it is? Bocconi is more part of the global job market.
Yes, exactly.

If you want to get a job at Bocconi, coming here doesn't make sense; they pretty much only hire from abroad.

But would it help you get a job in Rome, for example?
Actually, it could. There are connections of professors here with professors in other departments. I don't know how objective I can be since I don't know other Italian universities. But it is not impossible to move from Bocconi to another Italian university.

9. Stockholm School of Economics interviews

There are two interviews with Stockholm School students. The first interview was with a woman from Eastern Europe and a man from Sweden. The second interview was with a female Swedish student and a male student from another European country.

INTERVIEW 1

How did you end up coming to Sweden?
I did my undergraduate degree in economics in the US. Then I worked at a consulting company for a year. I applied to a variety of graduate schools, and this was the best offer I got. Initially I did not expect that I would continue teaching. Instead, I expected to go to an international institution such as the IMF or the World Bank.

I only applied to the two schools in Stockholm because I had family reasons to live in Stockholm. I was considering other European universities.

How did you judge among the different European universities?
I followed standard reputation and talked to my adviser. By reputation, I'd say Pompeu Fabra, Barcelona, LSE, UCL [Université Catholique de Louvain], and the Stockholm School of Economics rank in the top five in Europe. In some of them, however, you had to take a Masters program before entering the PhD program, and no one could give you guarantees about entering the PhD program. [Editor's note: that has since changed at many schools.] Here you did not. I heard that in one school only about 30 percent of the students actually pass the PhD program mainly because the school does not have room for them in the PhD program.

Would the education you received have been different if you had gone to any of the other schools?
I think there would have been some difference. When I started the program, I was expecting more courses in international economics. But due to some political considerations they're not offering the course in international

economics here anymore. I think they're very flexible here; in some cases that is good and in some cases it isn't.

I'm sure it would have been a big difference if, say, I had gone to a US school. When I was applying, I was looking for a US-style PhD program. Much of my decision rested on financing and scholarships.

Do foreign students get support here?
Yes.

I think we're pretty much on equal terms.

Do private universities differ from public universities?
In Sweden, we have a good example: Stockholm University, which is public, and the Stockholm School of Economics, which is private. In the private university students don't get four years of financing directly, which they do at public universities. Here, for example, you have to apply for a fellowship each year. Another difference is that you get employed by the university after the third year at a public university, which means you have to pay taxes on your "income." But, you also have access to government subsidies that private students don't. Those are pretty much the main differences.

How many students enter the program?
There are about 12 students each year. In my year, there were six in economics and six in finance.

We were eight in economics, two in statistics and another three in finance.

Are the classes only about 11 or 12?
No, initially we take classes together with the University of Stockholm so the classes are larger. There are also students from other schools taking courses here. A number of programs between the two are joint. So in the first year the classes are about 30, but then they get much smaller. There is an institute here and most of the professors from the University of Stockholm who teach in the joint program are members of the institute.

What's the attrition?
In economics maybe one or two will drop out. Of the two who dropped out my year one went to the US and one went to the private sector. Those two were in the university, not the Stockholm School of Economics.

Why do people drop out?
In my experience they've never been pushed out, they've chosen to leave. They were both women who left; one left because she got a job at a research institute and another left because she had a child.

What's the division between men and women and Swedish and non-Swedish students?
About a third of the students are women at both schools. Swedish students make up about half the students. They need Swedish-speaking students because they need teaching assistants and the undergraduate courses are taught in Swedish. (There is one undergraduate course taught in English.)

Can you describe the typical program?
All the courses in the first year are mandatory. We have quarters here and a quarter is about a month and a half. The mathematics class was based mainly on lecture notes. Micro 1 covered general equilibrium and was based on Mas-Colell. Micro 2 covered game theory and I–O, and was based on Laffont. Almost all teachers hand out lecture notes. In macro, most recently they only used lecture notes. In my year we used Blanchard/Fischer.

How do they judge your mastery of the material?
We have problem sets and exams. The exams follow the problem sets very carefully. The problem sets are a good guide to the central ideas. Usually the problem sets are more difficult than the exams. There are no general exams. The grades are distinction, pass, and fail.

Do the grades matter much?
It does matter because if you want to go on an exchange program your grades and recommendations are important. The professors can distinguish between various levels of pass, and how you compared with other students. Five years after graduation they won't matter. They are, however, a signal for the academic community. And people care about them.

The third year consists mainly of thesis work. In the second year courses, there is more flexibility because the courses are small. They want you to start the thesis work earlier but often it is an abrupt change. There are papers in many of the second year courses. And often you can discuss with the teacher whether you want an exam or paper.

Are most dissertations a monograph or a collection of essays?
In 1994 they changed the program to be a US-style program, and since then articles have been the main thesis structure.

Turning to general economic issues. Is there such a thing as mainstream economics and if so what is it?
I have a personal view on that. Mainstream economics is primarily what non-mainstream economists call neoclassical economics. Unfortunately, it is not easy to define neoclassical economics. There really is no theory of neoclassical economics; it is more a set of tools. It started with Walras and the Austrian school. I also consider Keynes a neoclassical economist. It is the tradition that's taught at every top university.

Where would behavioral economics fit?
I don't know how I classify them.

I think it's harder to specify a particular mainstream economics; there's something very dynamic in economic thought. It is constantly changing. Of course, there are the main ideas such as those held by the people that he mentioned.

What are the differences between European and US economics?
One difference between Europe and the US is that the academic tradition here in Europe is more open to a wider-ranging discussion, and more radical viewpoints. It is not a problem taking courses in, say, classical economics. European universities are more connected to the world. You can get that in many schools in Europe, although not in this particular school because this program is very US style. I think that the historical perspective on economics characterizes much of European economics and that is not part of the US-style programs.

Actually, here in Europe that part of the program is being abandoned. For example, there was a course held here called economic history that was compulsory for the students. The course counted for three credits whereas most classes counted for five credits, but it was required for all graduate students. They're not offering that course anymore because they consider it unimportant. The openness of the faculty here to taking such courses is small. I think part of the reason is that they think the program here has to follow the US-style and structure. In a sense, getting specific is very good. However, I think that as a social scientist you should have a point of view of society, so yes economics is opening a door to psychology now, but it is closing many others.

Economics is structured a lot around math. Do you find it useful?
I think the maths are useful. In the absence of a clear methodological rule math provides a useful structure.

For me it was a challenge in the beginning of the program because it was a very different level math than what I have experienced before. But I started realizing that it is useful because it gives structure. For example, when somebody suggests that a process moves in a certain way, math lets us clarify precisely what is meant.

Does economics have a political orientation?
I think math is used as a political tool to justify decisions of government policy. I personally think that is not what should drive economics although in many cases that is what happens. People want to prove that something is beneficial. They start with what they want to prove, as opposed to trying to see how a certain policy affects society.

I read a book on methodology and the vague idea I got about classical and neoclassical economics is that classical economics discusses value and neo-classical economics discusses price. It depends what aspect of the market you're focusing on—production or price. It's all very political.

What is the political orientation of most economists?
It was interesting reading the abstract of the paper you are presenting tomorrow where you found that the US economists were actually liberal. I had thought that in terms of economic policy US economics students are more conservative, or laissez-faire.

I agree. If you look at how finances are managed in the world, and you recognize that there are economists behind that, you conclude that they're pretty conservative. Market solutions are encouraged.

What is the political orientation of the school here?
I haven't noticed.

I think the professors are pretty neutral. Professors here, at least under-graduate level, avoid discussing politics in the classroom.

Would you discuss monetary or fiscal policy in macro?
Macro is pretty technical; they do not discuss examples from the real world. There is no discussion about what is better or worse. All you see are the equations. You can come to your own conclusions afterwards as to whether that equation applies to the real world or not. I know that they discuss politics a bit more at the undergraduate level. This is a business school and it is more acceptable to discuss politics at that level. In the graduate program, they want to give us a theoretical aura about policy problems but they don't discuss policy.

What makes a successful economist?
Technical skills are an important part of it. You also need a lot of knowledge about politics and institutions, and a lot of empirical knowledge about the economy to be a good economist.

Do you get that in your training?
The latter are not part of the training; they expect you to collect that by yourself.

I agree. In grad school only the technical skills are very important; you need those skills to see patterns that you can actually describe. For me, a good economist would be a person whose work actually can be used for policy, and is not just a fancy model that is far away from reality. A good economist has to have the ability to see how the real world works, and apply the knowledge gained to real-world phenomena.

Do you get any training in how the real world works?

[Laughter]

No, not really.

Do you receive any guidance in how to relate the tools to the real world on your own?
If the questions is, do we receive any formal training in applying the tools the answer is no. But we do it on our own. Part of it is finding a good adviser who's very good at interpreting social phenomenon.

How about formal training in methodology?
There was an optional course at a university but it didn't get at what most of us were interested in.

Let's talk about past economists. Would you ever study any Joan Robinson?
I know who she is but nothing about her.

I don't know who she is.

How about Keynes?
We talk about new Keynesians here. There is no discussion of Clower, Leijonhufvud, or any post-Keynesian macro.

We've never talked about Keynes here in any class.

How about Gunnar Myrdal or Friedrich Hayek?
Students know Myrdal here because he is Swedish, but he is really not discussed. We know a little bit of the newest Hayek, but we don't discuss him either.

English is now the language of economics. Neither of you are native English speakers. How much of a cost do you believe that poses for you?
I don't see it as a burden. I feel very comfortable working in English.

I think that it lowers my productivity, perhaps by 10 percent, 15 at the most. Since I did my undergraduate work in English when I try to say something that is related to economics in my native language I have a hard time.

Actually, I started learning economics in a third language, Spanish, and am more comfortable in Spanish than in English. In any case I'm more effective writing in Spanish than in English. The mathematics doesn't matter what language it is.

Would non-English-speaking students be more comfortable in a technical course with lots of mathematics?
That's an interesting idea. I suspect it's true, especially for Asian students. Sometimes when talking to Asian students they do not understand what they're saying, but their math is outstanding.

Do economists agree on issues?
I think that there is a set of topics that they agree on, but there are also topics on which economists disagree.

There is disagreement, of course. There's always disagreement about how to interpret results, interpret data, and what conclusions to draw from the data. The one discussion, which is the main discussion in economics, involves technical disagreements. But you also have ideological disagreements. But that's not so common in academia.

Where will most of the students go when they graduate?
Some will go to the central bank; others to some research institute. Still others will stay in academia. There's a whole variety of places that they go. In terms of geography, most students are very mobile. I suspect that European PhD students are more willing to leave Europe or their countries than US students are.

A lot of students here, if they get the money, go to school and the US for a year, and attend the US schools as a special student.

INTERVIEW 2

How have you liked the program so far?
I've liked it.

In general I've liked it, but I've had some problems because I wanted to do it part-time, which is not something that the program favors.

What are the strengths and weaknesses of the program here?
One strength is the cooperation with the University of Stockholm's program. That adds both breadth and depth to the program.

Another strength is that we have many American professors giving lectures here and giving many courses here. It might have something to do with the fact that the Nobel Prize home is here.

Stockholm is part of the ENTER consortium. Have you had any involvement with that?
Not really. We've been told that even if you do a visiting year in the US you can still spend a semester attending another school at the consortium.

Do people go to the US a lot?
If they do, that's definitely seen as positive.

Why is it seen as positive?
Because it is going to the research frontier. You can really see what was going on.

In general, changing environments serves a useful purpose, but you always want to step up in the rankings when you visit somewhere. So the best schools in the Nordic countries are not going to be the best schools in the world.

Will you both go over?
I'm in the process of applying now.

What would you define as mainstream economics?
Everything is more or less mainstream. There's nothing really unorthodox anymore. Becker is a pioneer. I guess some of the new economics still is not mainstream, but it will be eventually.

I still think that even if behavioral economics is coming, it is still only semi-mainstream now. I'm into experimental economics and sometimes I get reactions that suggest that it is far from mainstream.

Is there an experimental lab here?
There isn't a formalized lab, but there's a team here that is part of a European network that also includes Harvard, Princeton, and MIT that focuses on the advancement of behavioral economics. So in that sense behavioral economics is definitely an important research topic here among students and faculty. But up until now, it's been more the traditional paper-style experiments rather than computer-style experiments.

Is there too much or too little math in the program?
I don't think there's too much. I did math as undergrad, but I wasn't really prepared because the math used here is different. I had focused on linear algebra and combinatorials, which I really enjoyed. Then I came here and there was a lot of real analysis. So I was just a bit overconfident before I started, which gave me some difficulty.

For me it was the opposite. My undergraduate work in economics did not contain math at all. I found the math structure here helpful. It lets you repeat the analysis and cement your knowledge. So I don't think that training was a problem. It could be a problem if we get to the point that the only way we can do economics is by using math. I'm not sure math is always best way to solve world problems.

Where I studied in Europe in my undergraduate economics course I had to read the classics—Marx, Schumpeter, Hayek. I enjoyed that, and I think it served an important purpose. It is nice to know all that.

I think that some more interdisciplinary flexibility would be good. Then one could choose a course like that. I think most students would agree with that. I know some students wanted to go do more math, which they did at the Royal Institute of Technology [Stockholm]. I think that as long as one gets the core tool work, there should be flexibility at the margin.

Would most students agree with that?
I think so.

What's the political orientation of the students and the department here?
I think it's pretty center in terms of Swedish politics. I consider myself somewhat right wing, not libertarian, but conservative. I'm more classical liberal and I'm in the minority here both among students and faculty.

I would say that the variances are much smaller than the population. You can't really use the American or British framework. Compared to the Swedish population, Swedish economists, both students and faculty, are slightly more to the right. You have the social democrats, but you don't have the left-wing social democrats among the students.

It's somewhat more difficult to say with the faculty. Students don't discuss politics with them and we don't get politics in the classroom, whereas students discuss among ourselves all the time. But my guess would be that the faculty's politics is about the same as the students.

I would agree with that, but we don't discuss policy at all in the classes.

Are you unhappy that you don't?
Yes, but that might just be of reflection of the first-year classes, which are totally technical. I hope there will be room for it in the upper-level classes.

In the electives that I've chosen there hasn't been any discussion of policy.

That's why you don't need a broad knowledge of economics to succeed as an economist, which to some extent is really bad. You don't have to follow the public debate in any subject. Maybe this is good science, but I'm not sure. The environment attracts people who are not really interested in the public debate on policy. Since I enjoy policy and politics a lot, I miss it. This environment doesn't attract that kind of person.

I definitely agree. For me it is also a problem since my goal is not teaching. I don't want to become a professor.

Did you put that on your application?
Actually, I do want to do the teaching part; I just don't want to get into the research part. So, in my application, I did mention that I wanted to teach, but I strategically did not emphasize it, so they probably missed that. But I did discuss the possibility of going into an international organization.

Do they value certain goals that differ from the students' goals?
I think it's clear that they want us to stay in academia and do research. But I haven't really had that discussion with any faculty yet.

I've had a discussion indirectly. I wanted to go half-time and only have my funding come half-time. Both the implicit and explicit arguments have suggested that the problem with this is that they do not want to create the program that is not optimized for academia. I have another colleague in the program who wanted to do a longer internship, and that was discouraged as well. So I would say that there definitely is a bias towards academia.

Do economists agree or disagree on issues?
Disagree.

Early on in my undergraduate career I would have said that they agree, whereas now what I see are primarily arguments. Perhaps I'll go into another phase where I will see the agreement. I'm not sure what my final answer will be.

On the survey that you took, where would your answers to the monetary or fiscal policy questions have come from?
Definitely not from my courses here. Some came from my undergrad courses and some came from general reading.

I would agree, although I would add that some of my views have changed from informal discussions with fellow students.

How much of your education comes from your classes and how much from just interaction with students and informal reading and discussion?
I've learned a lot more about tools from the program. But when it comes to what's happening in terms of research, or how the economy really works, it has come from my discussions with colleagues or from my own reading.

I think that captures a problem with the education we can get. There are all kinds of interesting seminars going on here in Stockholm, but we're discouraged from attending them in the first year. The total focus is on getting the course work behind you. It is really only the third year when you start doing research that you are encouraged to attend seminars. I believe it should be more up to each student. I also believe that they encourage students to start research earlier. For example, in the finance part of this program here, students are encouraged to start research and thinking more broadly much earlier than in the economics part.

I agree. That's one reason why we take so long to get a degree. It is difficult for people to switch to research after having done the course work. I think you would be good to have more general courses and more papers early on.

I think moving out one or two of the courses from the first year to the second and third year would make the program more palatable and better integrate students into research.

10. Oxford interview

This interview was with four students, from different backgrounds including British, Western European and US. They are upper-level students in their third through fifth year.

INTERVIEW

There are four men here; would you consider yourself a representative sample of the department, and if not in what way would you differ?
Do we all know the department coordinator? [Laughter] [Editor's note: the department coordinator was extremely helpful in setting up the interviews.]

How did you get into economics?
I applied for politics, philosophy, and economics as an undergraduate study here intending to drop economics after my first year. But I really enjoyed the economics and carried on with it. I also enjoyed the philosophy, so I meandered into getting an MPhil in philosophy at another school where the MPhil was strongly economics based. Then I did some work in London, which was more economics based, so it was not such a jump into economics. Then I got a fellowship here at Oxford, and I came back here to do the MPhil and DPhil in economics.

I went into a program in economics and law. I enjoyed both, but I felt that I was more interested in the economics. I finished the degree and then I came here to do the MPhil and DPhil.

I went to an American university as an undergraduate. I wasn't certain that I was going into economics originally. I really enjoyed physics, but I did major in economics. After graduating, I wasn't really ready to consider graduate school. So I worked at a law firm for a while, because I was considering law. Working there, I decided I didn't want to do law, at least not contract law. I applied to Oxford for the MPhil, and then decided to stay for the DPhil.

When I finished high school, I didn't know what to do. It was by chance that I ended up in a social science university, and I was fascinated by economics from the first time I took the course. But then I became tired of economics, and I thought that everything was useless. So I took an MPhil in sociology, politics, and general social sciences. Then, I went back to economics because I ultimately decided that economics was slightly better to my way of thinking. I did some policy work back home, and then decided to continue my studies. I decided on Oxford because of the college system they have here. I like the way Oxford works, but at the same time, I wanted some kind of American program—where you have two years of courses plus three years to work on the thesis.

Did you consider other schools?
No, because I was already here.

I had a scholarship specifically for Oxford, and before that I knew that I was interested in studying economics.

I applied to some other schools in the US, but they were macro oriented, and my background didn't fit well there. Apparently, Oxford liked my micro focus.

I wanted to spend time in Europe so I considered European universities, and the top US universities.

Where does Oxford rank in the British and the global ranking system of graduate economics programs?
It all depends upon the topic. I do economic history, and in this field Oxford is, in my view, the top department in Britain, and likely the top department in Europe. In econometrics or micro, it also ranks quite high.

I don't have much basis for comparison, but I think the micro is strong. It has been challenging, and I get support whenever I need it.

I don't know in a quantitative sense, but I think the canteen discussion tends to go exactly along those lines—the general student seems to think that econometrics and development are strong, and maybe micro as well, that Oxford is "up there." I don't know about other fields.

I disagree with that somewhat. There are lots of quantitative rankings out there, and I'm not sure whether you are asking about those rankings or about what we perceive about quality.

How you interpret the question is as interesting to me as what your answer is. For example, at LSE, it was quite clear that the students had their own set of rankings, and those were used very quantitatively. Would you say that that suggests a difference between Oxford and LSE?

There could be a difference in job market focus. I don't know whether any of us are on the job market now; that makes a big difference in how we answer this question. You start thinking about these things most when you are on the job market.

When do you start thinking about the job market?
I think Oxford doesn't focus much on the job market through your career here. At some point you might say to someone that you are thinking about the job market, and they will help you think about it, but they definitely don't start focusing on it at the beginning of your studies. Other places do a bit more.

I agree with that. I don't know people at LSE, but I think that that makes intuitive sense. I also have the feeling that people I am working with are not happy with that. I haven't thought much about how something I might do might affect my CV.

There was a seminar sometime last year when they talked about the job market for the first time. I was a little scared, because I found out that I might not have good job potential because I'm doing something that's not applied. But I haven't thought about it since then. I just have been doing my work.

I know some people at LSE so I can do some comparison. I feel that they are building up people for the job market. Besides that, I don't think the quality of the education is much different, although the way the Oxford system is structured in terms of teaching is not exactly the same. I think that at LSE the professors are more on top of the students than they are here. Here, education is slightly more hands-off.

In the US, students told me that if the professor thought that they were not going to a top academic job, he or she would give us very little time; they wouldn't want to spend time with such a student. Would that be consistent with what happens here?
I am active in the job market now. I have had to push people to help me here. There's no worry by the teachers about what you are going to do.

I have a story that's been on the grapevine that certain supervisors have that mindset, and that some are quite agnostic about what students do.

I feel that I get a lot of attention, and they don't know whether I'm going to be an academic or not.

In my book on graduate economic education in the US, I described the system as producing efficient journal article writers. From what I'm hearing

that's not what the education is here. If you were to capture in one sentence what they are trying to produce here, what would that sentence be?
I'd say that they are producing economists. I know that sounds vacuous, but in fact, it suggests that their mindset is very general. That means that if you want to be an academic economist, a policy-maker, or go to work for an investment bank, that's fine. This is consistent with the general Oxford ethos—you read what you want, you learn what you want, and we'll push you in economics, but beyond I think they really are agnostic as to what we do.

[Others agree]

Now that we've heard the stories from each of you, would you say that you are representative? If I had four randomly selected students, would I find similar views?
You would probably have one woman.

Would having a woman here lead to different answers?
The graduate student body here is diverse; we are diverse, so in that sense, we probably are representative.

I think you are missing a student who went straight from undergrad to the DPhil, but their view probably wouldn't differ much from ours.

We only have one British student here. A matched sample would probably have two British students and two foreign students.

Could you describe a general day for you—from the time you get up to the time you go to bed?
It depends on whether you mean on term or off term. and what year you are. I am a fifth year student. On term, I would spend a lot of time preparing my teaching, or marking papers. One or two times a week, I would have a seminar or workshop. I would prepare my teaching. From time to time, I'd work with data from my thesis. Off term, or terms when I don't teach, I spend much of my day in front of the computer.

I wake up at 7:45am, go eat breakfast. and then work on my thesis until lunch. I eat lunch with random academics, not only economists, then after that I work on grading papers—often all afternoon until dinner time—dinner is with my wife. Afterwards, I work on stuff not directly related to my thesis, but still economics for maybe an hour or two; then I go to bed.

I wake up and come in at 9:00 or 9:30am, and then sit in the library and work on my thesis. I will do that for most of the day. I'm doing two elective papers, but they are subjects that don't have a lot of lectures to go to, but they do have some. Then I have dinner, and try to do a bit more work. Then I go to bed.

I have quite a lot of flexibility in my schedule, but on a typical day when I'm not teaching I come in at about 8:00am and mess around with equations or otherwise work on my thesis. I go to lunch at college, and try to find a lunchtime seminar that interests me. Then I work on my thesis until about 6:00pm or so.

Would you do it again?
[All agree yes, they would]

Would you do it again at Oxford?
[All agree yes]

Can you describe what you learn in the micro, macro, and econometrics sequence?
In micro we have both a market-based approach and a game-theory-based approach. The way the exams are structured lead students to focus on one approach or another. In the market approach they cover risk and uncertainty, general equilibrium, public goods and externalities. There is a different teacher for each of the different units. They all have their own takes on the issues.

Do you use a textbook?
No, Mas-Colell is sitting there for the market portion but it's not as though the course is taught out of the textbook.

In macro, it starts with an overview of the macroeconomic debate reviewing the New Classical and New Keynesian approaches. Then you go on to talk about growth theory, the real business cycle approach, consumption theory, optimization and overlapping generations, and then towards the end, the course tends to go a bit more toward the Keynesian approach, talking more about policy. Before that they talk about micro foundations. Then, last year they had a section on monetary economics.

Would they talk about monetary and fiscal policy?
Yes, you get a distinct section on policy, and monetary policy issues in particular.

In the US the students said that they never mentioned monetary or fiscal policy in their macro classes. So I guess that isn't a description of the situation here?
[All agree that that is not the case here]

There's a two- or three-week section on Taylor rules. We started with a simple model of the economy, determining the optimal monetary policy there, and then we made it more complicated.

During our year, we did dynamic stochastic general equilibrium models that are strictly policy.

I think that the micro and macro courses are more like snapshots rather than organized courses. There are good people who work in subfields, and they teach their stuff.

If what you are getting are snapshots, how do you prepare for the exams?
The way the exams are arranged here allows you to specialize. You get lots of choice in the exam. Out of 10 or 15 questions, you choose three. So when you study you prepare only a set of topics.

I feel like there is a difference in the lack of a textbook in macro versus micro. In micro there is at least one—Mas-Colell. In macro, there is nothing holding it together.

I think the first year micro is the same here as in the US. We probably do a bit less of the general equilibrium market stuff, and a bit more of the game theory. Macro is, I think, a bit more idiosyncratic. People talk about what their research interest is.

I got the impression that the payoff for students is to pick a certain number of topics and try to cover that topic very comprehensively, so you know all the key authors and issues in that topic, but not to cover two topics half as well. If you prepare an extra topic or two, then even if the question is from the periphery of that topic, you will still be able to do it. That's the case particularly in macro. You don't think about relations of topics.

In the US, the qualifying exams were sometimes described as "problem-set lite," by which was meant that they were easier versions of the problem sets. Would that be a description of the exams here?
I don't think that the exams would be described as easier than the problem sets. We get problem sets, and looking at past exam questions, they are as hard or harder than those we get on the problem set. But you don't have to answer all of them.

The questions are divided into essay and problem, or math, questions. You have to answer three questions with at least one from each section. I think the most common is to take two essays and one problem.

The problem sets tend to focus almost exclusively on the maths, so the exams add a new component. Within the topic areas if you have thought well about how, say, the Romer growth model interacts with the Lucas growth model and the Solow growth model, that kind of crossover is well rewarded in the essay in a way that is never mentioned in the course or a problem set.

In the US, the person who makes and grades the exam is the person who gave the lecture. I take it that that isn't the case here?
That is not the way it is here. I actually prefer it the way it is here. It means I don't have to obsess so much about idiosyncrasies, or about what a specific lecture meant. I can focus more on the general message. It also gives you more scope to look at different papers or look at a different text.

The questions are generally set by the lecturers; it is only the grading that is done by someone else.

I think it is important that it includes an outside reader.

It does, however, put more pressure on you in the sense that you can't game the style of answer to give. For me it was quite hard to adapt.

In the US students get very little training in economic history or economic thought. Do they get much training here in those areas?
There is only one course in history of economic thought, and normally it is taken by two people out of the whole community. There is a lack of interest in it. Here we have both an MPhil and a PhD, and about 50 percent of the MPhils are not going on to do a PhD.

I think that there is a feeling that because so few people do it, that it is not mainstream. There is also a feeling that it is not rigorous.

In the last three or four years, students have been taking the course in economic history as an applied macro course. It allows them to practice the tools in econometrics that they have been learning.

Let's talk about your training in econometrics.
It depends on who is teaching it. There's a lot of focus on different techniques. Last year in the first term there was a big focus on maximum likelihood. Then in the second term, we did a four-week unit on time series, and then a four-week unit on cross-sectional. The first two weeks concerned instrumental variables; the second two weeks covered non-linearities like logit and probit.

I think the attitude here is to concentrate on getting the theory right. Lots of people had no statistical background when coming here, so they are teaching you from scratch. The second term is a bit more applied, but it is still quite theory heavy.

I think econometrics is probably the most coherent of the three courses.

Yes, I agree, the econometrics sequence progresses very well.

What happens in the second year, when you are still in the MPhil, but are preparing for the DPhil?
There is both a thesis and two courses that you have to take. In terms of your mark; the courses count for two-thirds and the thesis counts for one-third. If you plan to stay on for the doctorate, the thesis is more important.

Is the thesis seen as the beginning of your PhD thesis?
In many cases, it is. It often makes a chapter.

What is the structure of most of the PhD theses here? Are they three essays, or are they single topics?
Most people go for the three essays. Sometimes people will structure it as having chapters, but even these will often be three essays. It's quite rare that you get a coherent book as a thesis.

What is your view of behavioral economics?
I think it's interesting, but there isn't any smoking gun of great insights that comes out of it.

I'm looking into fuzzy logic and digital applications, and I'd like to study some behavioral stuff, but I don't have time. I know the limitations of micro theory and the rational consumer very well. However, there isn't much done on behavioral economics here.

There certainly is not much experimental work being done. There is a sense that the faculty here is skeptical about it.

Is there a mainstream economics, and if so how would you characterize it?
I think from when I started economics in the 1990s, I had the idea that there was something called mainstream economics, but that is less the case here. There are many new fields now—like behavioral and experimental economics that are gaining in strength and adding new insights.

I think some fields remain somewhat heterodox—say econophysics. It is definitely not mainstream—it is taught in a physics department, not an economics department.

Heterodoxy in that sense is multiple agent models. Other than that I think modern economics is quite broad church.

I agree, but I still think that there is definitely a notion of heterodox out there. My old university was quite heterodox and there are a number of economists there who are quite skeptical about much of what is done in economics. They would question how much we can learn from math alone, and would argue that one needs more focus on actual human beings. My honors thesis was a multi-agent simulation of cooperation and altruistic behavior. To my knowledge, no one is doing anything along those lines here. Since I've come here I've fallen into the Oxford mindset, and am more skeptical of my undergraduate thesis. Having said that, it is still a field out there that no one here is doing.

Yes, that multiple agent work looks heterodox, and then there's people who just don't use math, which is also heterodox.

What's your reaction to heterodox economics?
I'm completely open to the multi-agent approach. I'm not particularly open to the "no math" approach. Math is just a part of language.

I find it difficult to read, say Joan Robinson, where you are expressing quite complicated ideas without using any equations. But is that a failing of mine, or is it a failing of Joan Robinson? Probably the former.

I think there are a lot of articles that are basically conveying insights that could be expressed verbally, but at the same time. The math is probably what makes the discipline rigorous.

Would the others of you have read Joan Robinson?
We have heard of her, but have not read her.

How about John Hicks and Friedrich Hayek?
Hicks's work was instrumental in my interest in economic history.

What's the difference between normative and positive economics?
I understand the basic issue. We talked about social welfare functions in micro, but I'm not prepared to actually sit down and talk about the broader issues of policy.

I think the distinction is valuable; something can be done with it. I guess the normative side of economics is not well developed in general.

The time I really encounter it is not when I'm reading papers or when I'm talking to faculty, but when I'm teaching students. With undergraduates you often can't talk about the maths, so you talk about the general bigger issues.

Is the economics profession heading in the right direction?
I think it is going in the right direction. I think that economics now is more open and willing to listen to other disciplines. That's good.

As long as we maintain rigorousness, and I don't think the profession is willing to sacrifice that; I agree.

I think I'd generally agree, but I'm disappointed that there is a lack of understanding and teaching of how we got to where we are. I feel like we are presented with the latest greatest theories, and we have no sense of the intellectual background, or of how someone like Adam Smith could have written such a wonderful treatise without doing it mathematically. My second concern is that sometimes there seems to me a sense in the profession that we can learn about the world from mathematics; I think mathematics is best done when mathematics is used to formalize and provide the rigor for an idea that could be expressed without mathematics. I sometimes get the impression that when we prove something, it's not just a proof given the assumptions, but that it actually tells us something about markets. Maybe there is no way of avoiding it given that we have to teach a rigorous graduate course in a short period of time.

I agree. I'm not entirely clear on the direction economics is headed. I also think it is important that an argument be rigorous—that it fits together properly, and math provides a way of ensuring that that's so. But you also need to be able to make the arguments without the math. You could view behavioral economics as a direction the profession is going—away from a particular model of human decision-making—but I'm not completely sure whether it is a direction or a fad.

I sometimes think of cycles—going from theory to empirical analysis. We had been going toward theory and now we're going toward empirical analysis.

One of the results of the survey was that there was less stress in European schools than there was at top American schools. Is that consistent with your sense?
I think most of the stress here comes from the exam in year three. That's the high point of the stress. What you don't have here is the aiming for the job market at the very beginning.

For the most part, I think that is right, but there are times of high stress, which are connected with exams and teaching and research.

Talking to some of my friends who are in graduate programs in the States, my sense is that they don't seem particularly more or less stressed than we are. We all have some work to do.

I think the first year of the MPhil here is stressful. I found, and I think I'm speaking for most students, that it's not just the lead up to the exam that is stressful. There is a discrete jump in the standard content. With no criticism of any individual, I think that sometimes the structures aren't there to support the students. I felt that many of the students were completely bewildered and no one wanted to be the one to say "Roll back five pages and tell me what they mean." What I'm saying is that it isn't the exams; the stress comes from two terms in which a lot of students, including the students who end up getting good marks, feel that they are out of their depth. I found that really stressful.

I think there is a big distinction between the teaching of undergraduates, where it is very close, where the number of students is small, and the graduate education here where you've got lectures of 50 people from senior faculty, then sections with the post-docs going through the math proofs. It not well designed to pick up any problems, particularly if those problems are that people are just feeling a bit lost.

At my old university, and other universities that I know of, if you fail your exams, or you get sick and can't take it, you don't have to wait six months. You can do another version of a similar, but sufficiently different, exam after a month or two. One student's father died three months before the exams, and he failed and they didn't let him take another after a couple of months. I think that was wrong.

I notice a lot of you talk about teaching here. Is that an important part of the education you're getting?
I think you could get away here without teaching a single class. I don't think that is as likely to happen in the US. Most PhD students there are doing some teaching. While I do a lot of teaching, I don't think I am representative.

I teach a lot as well.

I teach one class a year. It depends on your funding rate. I actually find teaching quite valuable, but I agree that it is possible to do too much teaching.

It keeps you in touch about what people who aren't economists think.

You actually start understanding things.

[Laughter]

How much interaction with other students besides economists do you have?
That depends a lot on the college that you are at. In Nuffield, they make you pay for lunch, so I try to eat there. They are all social scientists there, so I talk to other social sciences, but not to students in other fields as much as the others probably do.

For me it is lunch where I interact with non-economists.

How many hours a week do students put in, and does it vary by year?
My first year I didn't do anything other than work. It was probably 60 or 70 hours a week.

During terms, that's about right. Terms are short, and there is lots to learn. During breaks, I'd typically take two to three weeks off.

In the first year of the PhD after the Masters, I probably lowered it a bit, just to recover. Now I'm back into 70 hours per week.

I tried to keep myself on track in my third term by actually recording the number of hours a week I worked, stopping the timing if I got up and got a cup of coffee or anything like that. I didn't get up to 70 hours a week, but I agree with the others that it is about 60 hours a week. Basically, you feel that you are not doing anything else in your life than studying economics.

There are times when I am doing research where I will spend nine or ten hours in the office. But when things won't come, I sometimes surf the Internet, and that cuts down the amount of actual time working.

The second year is much the same, with the Masters thesis taking more time and the course work taking less time. We spent 21 hours a week in classes during the first year. Then the third year, there was a lull. I was still doing work, such as learning to program that I thought might be preparation for DPhil stuff, but it was not directly work on economics.

Where do you expect to be in five years, ten years?
My hope is to get a job in continental Europe.

I want to end up in academia, but it depends on what sort of results I get next year and a half.

I expect to still be doing economics, probably in academia or in some type of policy institute in Britain or North America.

I expect to be in the UK either in academics or in government.

11. Université Catholique de Louvain interview

This interview was with two women and one man. One was a third year student, one was a fifth year student and the third had just recently finished her dissertation and was a post doc student.

INTERVIEW

How did you make your decisions about applying?

I'm from Italy, and when I finished my undergraduate studies, I decided to get a closer involvement in neoclassical economics. I had to choose. On the one hand, there were the best heterodox universities to attend, such as the New School or Cambridge. On the other hand, there were the mainstream programs, and the European mainstream seemed more open-minded. It's not yet the pure American way. It's also cheap in Europe. The relationship between quality and cost here is good. At Cambridge or LSE, the tuition is much higher. In the US, it is also high, unless you get a fellowship. Here, all it costs is 800 euros tuition.

How do you finance your expenditures?

My family pays; once you start the PhD program, you get a fellowship.

When I finished my undergraduate work here in Belgium, I had no clue about what an MA or a PhD was. I discussed my future with a professor and he mentioned the MA, but I wanted to study abroad—primarily in the UK—but then I found that that was very expensive. I studied six months in Belgium and six months in the UK.

I went to Louvain for my Masters degree, since it is hard to find a job with just a Bachelors. Then I went on the job market, and didn't find anything that I liked, so I decided to do a PhD. But it was hard to start a PhD without redoing the two years of Masters courses. All schools in France and Spain wanted me to redo the two years of Masters courses. By staying here, I didn't have to redo most of it and just had to redo a few courses. I also received pay from the start, because I worked as a teaching assistant. That made it more like a job.

How many economics students are there in Louvain-la-Neuve?
In economics, there are about 50 or 60 PhD students and about 30 or 40 Masters students.

What percentage of the students who start a Masters go on for a PhD?
My guess would be that many do; it depends on the grade that you obtain; you need a distinction to go on for a PhD.

What is the nationality breakdown of the students?
Eighty percent Italian.

Maybe not quite that many, but there are a lot. That may be this year, but that is not normal.

Why so many Italians?
It is due to the problem with universities in Italy. It is also inexpensive here. Then there are some connections between some professors here with professors in Italy. Students come from all over Italy.

That's interesting; we had thought that they came from one or two places.

Are all graduate courses taught in English?
[In unison] Yes.

Does that fact that all graduate courses are taught in English present a problem for students who don't have English as a first language?
Most of the students speak pretty good English, and are comfortable with English. Sometimes the professors don't speak good English; that can be a problem. That's not many.

Can you describe the program here?
There is a large gap between the undergraduate and graduate program. It was amazing. In the graduate course I got no intuition at all in the core courses micro, macro, or econometrics; it was all math. It was not all that difficult, but it was just math. It was different in the field courses. At least that's what I remember.

Are problem sets important?
No.

What are the exams like?
What they ask from you is mostly mathematical skills. There is little intuition.

It's not really connected to policy issues.

My experience was a little different. My first macro class here was on growth theory; I had done my undergraduate thesis on growth theory, so I expected to know something about it. I didn't. The professor walked in and wrote a Hamiltonian on the board. It was a bit shocking. In macro, you get no clue about policy. Any clue that I got I got later studying by myself.

In micro, that's not true. In micro, we did a lot of game theory; that was fantastic—mechanism design. The general equilibrium studies were a mess; there was no intuition. I remember this hyperplane that separates everything from everything. You just memorize. If you had time to study it, it might have been better. Econometrics was just matrices. I remember that I could do everything with matrices; now I remember almost nothing. There was no practical econometrics in the core courses. In an upper-level econometrics course, we got more applied work.

Are the core courses taught by one professor, or by two or three different professors?
Micro and macro were taught by two or three. Econometrics was taught by only one.

Does the content of the courses change from year to year?
Yes, definitely. there is little consistency from year to year.

Louvain is known for general equilibrium, but almost none of the students here are doing it.

Do you do a lot of reading outside the courses?
I read a lot on my own once I finished the core, but when you taking the core courses, you spend all your time studying for them.

No, we had time to read besides studying.

Me too.

They are more intelligent than I.

You probably took a more concentrated load.

That's true; I also took history of thought as a fourth course.

It depends on your combination of courses.

How long does the core normally take?
We are required to take three one semester courses in micro, macro, and econometrics, but you can split them up and take them over an entire year.

In macro, the first semester is required; it is growth theory. The second semester is real business cycles; it is not required.

How long do most students stick around here?
In your first year here, you have to think of a dissertation topic by the end of your first semester. It really isn't much. You pick an article, and write some things about that article.

How large are the classes?
There are 30 or 40 students in the core courses.

And there are no problem sets?
No, there are problem sets; they are just not very important.

Does the exam follow closely after the problem sets?
For econometrics, they were not, at least in my case. In macro the exams did follow the problem sets. Back when I did it the exam was oral; but now it is written so it may be different.

What's the difference between a Masters thesis and a PhD thesis?
The Masters thesis is more a class paper that reviews literature than it is an actual thesis.

How long is it?
In my case it was 35 pages, but some may go to 100 pages.

My Masters thesis was 60 pages.

After you finish your Masters thesis, what happens?
For the doctoral program you have to do four more courses, and these can be taken here or at one of the nearby schools. That flexibility makes it nice.

Louvain is part of EDP consortium. Do a lot of students participate in that?
We don't; only a small minority actually participates.

You need a high ranking to participate in it; and you need to take specific exams. For example, you need advanced macro II and advanced micro II. In my case, I didn't participate because I had chosen other classes.

How long does the class work take?
The requirements have been changing; I believe that it is 120 hours of class time total, which is 30 hours per class, so it is not actually four classes required now; it is simply that the class work must add up to 120 hours.

Clearly, that leaves you with quite a bit of time. What do you do with it?
It depends on whether you are a teaching assistant. If you are a teaching assistant, you spend a lot of your time teaching.

What do you mean "a lot of your time"?
It means 180 hours in the class per year. You have to prepare problem sets and exams. Usually, you are a teaching assistant for several professors. Often the classes have 300 in them so with 25 in each tutorial, that means that you have 12 tutorials for that class.

What does the TA do, and what does the professor do?
The TA primarily does tutorials in which you primarily do exercises.

How big are the undergraduate classes?
The tutorials are about 25 students; the class size varies. Typically, students will meet once a week with the professor in a two-hour lecture and once every two weeks with a tutorial.

Some have said that in teaching the material to undergraduates is where you really learn it. Do you find that to be the case?
I think I learned a lot by teaching the first two years. You learn the material better because you have to explain it.

How much did you learn from your fellow students, and how much did you learn from your professors?
I'd say 50–50.

Me too. There is a lot of cooperation among the students.

I'd say less, but I didn't do the Masters here.

There is little competition here. Some friends of mine who are studying in the US say that it is much more competitive, and the environment is a bit awful.

Are the students happy here?
We are. [The others agree]

If you had asked me in the Masters year, you might have gotten a different answer.

[Laughter]

I have heard from the students doing the Masters here that some are really disgusted with the amount of abstract work, and they really, really, want to stop.

There are actually only a few lectures that focus on mathematics. The lectures in the field courses are not that mathematical.

What happens to students when they graduate? If there are about 80 or 90 students in the program, how many come out each year with a PhD and what do they do?
It is a one-year Masters and a three-year PhD normally, so it generally takes four or five years. If you do a TA, it is usually six years.

When do you start writing the PhD dissertation?
I was slow choosing a dissertation topic, because I was a TA, which took a lot of time. I switched a number of times—I started with trade, but it was too much involved with abstract models, so I switched to applied econometrics and education. I researched the literature, but I got no guidance on what was and wasn't being done, or any indication about what was the required level to publish. I really did the first paper almost completely on my own.

I read a lot, and there were some seminars where students presented papers to other students. I did get some guidance from professors.

I have not yet chosen a dissertation topic.

What is the nature of the dissertation?
It is generally three or four papers.

In some European schools, the papers are jointly written with the professor. Is that the case here?
Yes, you need at least one written on your own. The joint work doesn't have to be done with the professor; for example, I wrote with other students.

Does writing a joint paper result in any conflict of interest?
I wrote with my professor; it was nice to be treated as a young colleague. For me, it was a good experience. You learn how to focus on the idea and express it properly. I get tired of my work in two or three weeks, and it is nice to pass it off to someone else, and work on something else. I like collaboration.

I would have liked to have done a joint paper with someone good in my field. You go much faster.

Where do you see the field of economics?
In a blind alley. Especially in macro. I work in the history of economics, and I do macro economics. The impression I have is that there are two

types of economics—stuff from a model, in which you derive some conclusion from this model, and then try to figure out some policy implication. If you find something counterintuitive, you say that this is very good research, but often it is just a stupid result because the model is wrong. The other way to do research is to try to formalize something that we already know. There is a lot of research in macroeconomics that tries to explain the development of capitalist societies, or even the development of humankind from 2000 before Christ to present. And it is simply putting well-known ideas in formulas. I know that's a controversial view, but it's the way I see it.

I'd agree about macro. I'm working on applied econometrics, and I really get the impression that the models we're using are flawed. You get very complicated mathematical models, and when you get what the intuition is, you say, "We already know this." But in applied econometrics, I am much more enthusiastic about the work; we are becoming better and better at analyzing data. We have better and better computers and better and better methods.

I agree.

I'd prefer if we looked at reality and tried to explain that.

Would the three of you be representative of the students here?
My view is that we are less mainstream.

If I had more mainstream students here, how might the responses differ?
You're missing CORE [Centre for Operations Research and Econometrics] students, who focus on game theory. I would say that the people in industrial game theory would say that it's true that macroeconomics has serious problems. The concern about macro is shared by most students.

But they would be very enthusiastic about work being done in industrial organization.

What is the relationship between CORE and the university?
Which relationship?

There is not much interaction. They focus more on theory; they don't have applied econometrics there. However, if you are working on a topic similar to theirs, they are open to discussion.

Where would students there get their PhD from?
They get their PhD from both.

Is history of economic thought a subject here?
In the other program they have to choose—either they do history of economic thought, or they do economic history. Here both are offered.

When you finish your PhD, what happens to most students at that point?

[Laughter]

I'm laughing because when I finished I had no clue about the job market. I don't know how the job market works here. We had no clue about how the US market works for professors until we had a lecture about how it works. We saw it as another world. I don't know how it works in Europe. There is now a market in Spain that is close to that in the US. [Editor's note: that market has now become the European job market.]

Don't you worry about what you will do once you graduate?
Definitely.

[Laughter]

I have a deadline on my fellowship.

We are very worried.

What strategy do students have?
I can only talk about mine.

I'm sending some applications now, but these are general applications. Until you have a PhD there is little sense in sending anything out. Here in Europe, personal relationships mean much more in determining who gets what job. In Italy that is definitely the case. If you are outside the system, it is unlikely that you will get a job.

Are the job markets internal to the specific countries, or is there more of a European job market?
When you finish your PhD, you can apply all over Europe.

But some countries are more open than others.

In the US there are job placement officers to help students. Does that exist here?
There is nothing like that here. All the work about job searches we have to do ourselves. At best, you might get some help from a professor who knows someone who knows someone.

So is it fair to say that they graduate people and then leave you on your own?
[In unison] Yes, definitely.

I had no idea about how the job market worked, but I presented a seminar some months ago at a French university. They called me, and asked whether I wanted to have an interview there, so I was not very stressed. I wrote to Canadian schools about possibilities in Canada, and they wrote back that I should go to the AEA meetings in San Diego. I wrote back that I didn't want to go there—why would I want to go to San Diego when I am applying for a job in Canada, and I got an e-mail back explaining to me the way the job market worked in the US. Now, I realize how funny it was that I had no clue about how the job market worked. Now there is some better information.

Any other comments or questions about the survey you took?
I found a number of the questions ambiguous. For example, if you asked me, what makes a successful economist, it could be interpreted in many different ways.

How did you interpret it?
I see a successful economist as not necessarily the same as a good economist. A successful economist is an economist who gains recognition from other economists. A good economist is an economist who knows how the economy works, and they are not necessarily the same.

I'd agree; I interpreted the question as good economist, because successful economist did not seem relevant to the answers. A good economist not only understands the economy very well; he or she also contributes to society as an economist.

Aren't the people who are successful as economists doing that?
Successful, to me, is associated with fame and money, which are not necessarily associated with contributing to society. I interpreted it as good; I didn't see the purpose of being successful if you weren't good.

On the political orientation question in the survey, I had to change the question for Europe because the words are used differently in the two countries. In Europe, the large majority considered themselves liberal; another third considered themselves moderate, and less than 10 percent who considered themselves conservative.
What do you mean by moderate?

Another ambiguous term—somewhere between conservative and liberal or left. Would you say that there are very few conservative students here?
Yes; most of the students I know are more left than moderate.

[All agree]

Does that carry out throughout Europe?
I only know some universities, but the ones I know I would say yes.

If you could change the education here, how would you change it?
I think the courses could involve less math, and more content.

We all agree on that.

Would all the other students agree?
[In unison] Yes.

The state of the art is such that we should know math. But we also need economists. Here there are a lot of engineers, who are essentially mathematicians; they feel they are economists and they are not; they are not able to understand an indifference curve.

Have students here read the literature, say Keynes?
I have because I took a history of thought course. Many of the students took the course, because in undergraduate work, there is a complete lack of training in any literature.

Would you have heard of the Cambridge controversy?
I'm Italian; I know everything about that.

I don't remember what it was, but I do remember hearing about it.

Would you call the economics you are learning neoclassical economics?
It's unclear what neoclassical economics means.

What are the top economic PhD programs in Europe?
LSE, Pompeu Fabra, Toulouse, Tilburg, and then probably Oxford and Cambridge, Paris, the Stockholm School, and Barcelona.

It depends on the particular area you are talking about, and the way in which you are going to characterize schools.

Did many people here go over and spend a year in the US as part of their education?
No, although some would like to.

Many students in Europe go on to post-docs after graduating. Is that seen as a temporary holding status until you can figure out where to get a job?
Post-docs are great, because you don't teach and can do your research.

I would prefer something more definite.

How do post-docs pay?
The post-docs here are nationally determined in a competition among different fields, and once you get one, it is for three years. You can go to different schools or stay at one school. It's not the university that pays; it is the national government.

PART 4

Conclusion

12. Conclusion: how should economists be "made"?

My interest in studying graduate economics education in Europe is not prurient. As should be clear from my introductory chapter, I have definite views on what graduate economics education should be. I study graduate economics education to try to understand better why it is the way it is, and how it can be changed. I am, however, no utopian reformer. I fully recognize that institutions do not change easily, and that there is an inertia in institutions. Generally, change occurs only when it is forced upon institutions from outside or inside pressure. For the US economics profession that means little change is to be expected. US programs are doing acceptably well, and they are unlikely to change.

The US economics profession will eventually change, though, because the development of alternative global economics will challenge US supremacy in graduate economics. To date, US programs have not faced serious global competition. However, over the coming decade the same global pressures that hit US manufacturing will likely hit US graduate economics programs. That pressure will force change in US programs as foreign students, who currently make up 60 to 70 percent of the demand for US graduate economics programs, start choosing to go elsewhere, not as their second choice, as happens now, but as their first choice.

Europe is of special interest because it is the most likely contender for dominance in global economics. European policy-makers are now making a push for European economics to regain the prominence it had in global graduate economics education before the World Wars when Europe was the center of global economics. With their common education policy, European policy-makers are putting pressure on various European economics departments to measure up globally, and to become competitive with US economics departments. This outside-the-university pressure for change in European graduate economics programs makes those European programs much more open to change than are US graduate economics programs. Change in European programs is going to happen. The question is: what will the nature of that change be?

To date, the push for change in European graduate economics programs has, in many ways, been rather myopic. Instead of thinking dynamically about how the economics profession is evolving in response to changing technologies, and designing its institutions to win out in the future, Europe seems to be pushing for changes that will get the incentives in the European research environment to more closely mimic those in the US economics profession. The thought is that by pushing for such changes, they can improve the European global performance. Students recognize that that is happening as comes across clearly in the interviews. The programs I surveyed aren't there yet (although they are further along than the large majority of European programs), but it is clear that that's what they are aiming for. The survey and interview results reported in earlier chapters suggest that it is possible for European graduate economics programs to replicate the United States's graduate economics system. At all the schools that I surveyed and interviewed, the core training students received was very similar to the training they would receive in the United States.

While the survey and interviews show that it is possible for European policy-makers to design their graduate economics programs after US programs, from my earlier discussion it should be clear that I do not believe that the changes that European programs are currently instituting are a good model for traditional European programs. The traditional European programs need change, but they need change that fits into their institutional structure. In my view, the "copy-the-US" path they seem to be following will not improve the situation and will likely make it worse for the traditional European programs.

The programs where I interviewed students are in various stages of globalization, or making themselves United States-like. The Université Catholique de Louvain is probably the least globalized, and LSE is probably the most. LSE is also the most successful. That isn't surprising. LSE has a long history of being a top global program in economics, and also has the advantages of being in a native English-speaking country and of being closely integrated with the Bank of England and the British Treasury. If it hadn't been the most successful, I would have been surprised.

The Università Bocconi, the Universitat Pompeu Fabra, and the Stockholm School of Economics are somewhere in the middle in terms of globalization, but they, too, are all special cases in that they, unlike most European universities, are private. As private universities, they have not had to deal with integrating the incentives for publishing with the traditions and institutions of the countries where they are located. This gives them more freedom in their operations.

Oxford is the outlier. It is somewhat globalized, but it has maintained more of its traditional nature, probably because of its long historical tradition and high standing and name recognition in academia. That has allowed it to remain somewhat more aloof to the globalization pressures. It retains elements of the traditional European approach to graduate education.

In this concluding chapter, I explain why I believe the US model is not a good model for the large majority of the traditional European universities, and give the broad outlines of a radical alternative model for reorganizing economics research in European universities. My alternative model will, I suspect, be far too radical for most of my readers, and I could have modified it and discussed less radical reforms that are more politically possible. I did not do so, since I felt that my alternative model of funding and guiding research has the advantage of presenting the research problem facing Europe within a quite different perspective than most economists and academics take.

My goal in presenting my alternative model is not to get it adopted, but instead, to get readers to think about the research problem in economics from that different perspective. My belief is that once one starts thinking about research from that different perspective, one can use that alternative as a reference point to develop alternative reform proposals that are more politically correct, and hence more feasible to implement and achieve the ends the proposal is designed to achieve, which is to get the majority of economists to focus more on hands-on policy and teaching-relevant research written for policy-makers and students, while leaving a smaller proportion of the profession to focus on scientific and hands-off applied policy research written primarily for other economists.

The structure of the chapter is as follows: I first discuss the problem of measuring economists' output, which is central to current reform proposals that are attempting to structure European programs like US programs. I then outline my alternative "market-based research funding solution" for funding academic economics research. I conclude with some suggestions about reform of European graduate economics education even if my more radical suggestion is not followed.

WHAT IS ECONOMISTS' OUTPUT, AND HOW DO YOU MEASURE IT?

The beginning point of thinking about reform of European graduate economics programs is thinking about what the output of the system is, and what it should be. Most US universities specify economists' output as involving three components: research, teaching, and service.[1] They leave open the relative importance of each of these measures in promotion decisions, in part because the departments' weights that are used in decisions on promotion and tenure generally differ from the funders' implicit weights, especially in public universities, which are in large part government- or tuition-funded. Presumably tuition funding is 100 percent for teaching; government funding is for all three components, although the weights have not been fully determined, and likely differ among different types of universities. It is my sense that, if asked, most US state legislatures, except in the case for a small number of top university programs, would favor more funding for teaching and service to community than is actually the case. (It is an open secret in the United States that universities transfer toward research those resources given by funding agencies for teaching.) There is usually some wording in most university by-laws that all three elements should contribute to promotion decisions, but in most US graduate economics departments, the sense I get from talking to economists is that research gets either the highest weight, or the entire weight subject to a minimum threshold of teaching ability. Economics research has come to be measured by quality-weighted journal article output. Global European universities are following this practice, and the practice is quickly spreading to traditional PhD granting, and to non-PhD granting, European programs. This means that changes in the European system are creating strong incentives for European academic economists to publish journal articles at all university levels.

In traditional European universities, incentives have been quite different. As pointed out by Frey and Eichenberger (1992, 1993) there are two major differences. First, the non-journal-article aspect of research is accorded far more importance in traditional European universities; far less emphasis is laid on preparing research for journals. Until recently, European academic economists haven't faced the "publish or perish" pressure that US academics face. Second, in Europe, service is considered not only at the department and university level, but also at the national level; in Europe there has been a strong tradition of professors playing active formal and informal roles in advising governments and in public debates. Frey and Eichenberger argue that compared with US economists, a larger percentage of European economists play the role of public intellectual and weigh in on public debates about policy issues. Whether these insights are correct or not, it is accurate to say that there has been far less push for journal article publication in traditional European programs than there has been in US programs.[2] The result is that the US-based economists, many of whom are non-US born, dominate the academic journals.

OBJECTIONS TO USING A JOURNAL ARTICLE METRIC AS A MEASURE OF ECONOMISTS' RESEARCH OUTPUT

The current push on European programs is to compete better with the United States on the journal article ranking metric. I have a number of objections to the use of this metric for ranking research. My first objection is that it will have costs in other dimensions of economists' output—dimensions on which traditional European programs have done well. The use of a journal article metric gives zero weights to large numbers of research activities that are central to new ideas developing. That zero weighting leads researchers away from these unweighted activities and toward weighted activities. It leads rational researchers to focus on small, journal-publishable ideas, and to de-emphasize large ideas that might be more interesting, and have a larger research payoff to society. It also leads researchers to worry less about what their research is contributing to knowledge or society, and more to whether their research is journal publishable.

When an economics academic system becomes almost single-mindedly focused on a journal article output metric, the publication of the paper becomes an end in itself. That has happened in the United States. Essentially, my conclusion in my most recent study of top US graduate economics programs (Colander, 2006, 2007) was that these graduate economics programs have become specialists at producing highly efficient journal article writers, but far less proficient at producing broad-based research economists or at producing economists who will be proficient at teaching undergraduates.

My second objection to the journal article metric is that a formal metric that allows rankings of output is not needed. The economics profession's activities are informationally small activities, where informal knowledge that active economists have of other active economists' work provides a better measure of an economist's and a program's output than will any ranking based on a formal metric. "In-the-know" economists' informal ranking supersedes any formal ranking. The quantitative metrics that underlie formal rankings either ratify previously held views, or, if the rankings don't match one's prior views, lead one to look for problems in the metrics.

My sense is that if a knowledgeable objective outside observer were to rank European economics with US economics, he or she would rank European economics much higher than its "journal article ranking" places it.[3] Where European economics would rank especially high is in some important cutting-edge research. As we have argued in *European Economics at a Crossroad* (Rosser et al., 2010, forthcoming) Europe has been at the forefront of the complexity revolution and in many of the new ideas that will likely become foundational for economics in the future.

The reality is that those economists who do path-breaking work in research worry very little about formal metrics—for example, the fact that Bill Vickrey published many of his papers in obscure journals did not stop the profession from recognizing his contribution with a Nobel Prize. Nor has it stopped recent top US economists from publishing popular books, even though those books do not count in the journal article metric as "research output." Steve Levitt, Richard Thaler, Ian Ayres, and Daniel Ariely have all made important contributions with their books, and are considered top economists. Where they stand in some journal article metric basically does not affect their reputations. Similarly, Greg Mankiw has published textbooks, and Tyler Cowen, Gary Becker, and Brad DeLong have made impacts with their blogs. The list could be extended significantly.[4] My point is that top economists worry little about any output metric; rather, they concentrate on influence.

Eventually, once a sufficient number of other top economists publish books, write blogs, or gain their prominence from textbooks, the ranking industry will catch up, and we will have "new metrics" that incorporate those other dimensions of research. These new metrics will feed back into incentives, and second-tier economists will try to move up in the new dimension of rankings. When that happens other economists will follow by copying what top economists have done so that they can improve their own ranking. But of course that misses the point—*rankings follow what top economists do; top economists don't follow rankings, and if an economist is worried about ranking, he or she is unlikely to be a top economist.* Top economists are worried about ideas and influence, both of which are developed in myriad ways.

My third objection to any strong focus on a single formal metric based on journal articles is that journal articles are obsolete. Today, in the economics profession, much of the debate about an idea occurs in the pre-working paper stage; the research workshops at top universities are more central to the spread of ideas in economics than are journals. If you are reading an idea for the first time when it is published in a journal, you are out of the informal research loop, and are probably at least two years behind specialists' thinking about the idea. In fact, I would argue that a paper has already had much of the influence it will have on cutting-edge researchers by the time it reaches the working paper stage. Today, publication in a journal is more often than not a tombstone, marking ownership of an idea, than it is an important method of communication among cutting-edge specialists. Today, were journal publication metrics not used for promotion and tenure decisions, many existing print, and even online, journals would disappear because they would be unnecessary.[5]

With the development of easy access to the Internet, the economics profession is ripe for a major change in the way it organizes the transmittal of information among its members and to the general public. Specifically, we can expect an ArXiv-type system to develop in the coming decade, and for journals to decrease even more in importance, as usage and viewing statistics supplement and replace publication-based statistics.[6]

My fourth objection to the use of a formal output metric based on journal articles is that that metric and the journal articles that incorporate it do not measure economists' research output in a meaningful way. The reason for that failure is that research output is a multidimensional concept, and journal article output measures only a small part of the total; thus, it biases the research done to emphasize that particular dimension. Research includes working on an idea in one's mind, taking part in an online debate, developing new ideas, writing a book, taking part in a workshop, commenting on a paper in a workshop or online, editing a journal, refereeing, or developing some idea within a business. When an economist works with a local agency to figure out a better system of organizing its incentive system, that is research. When Fischer Black worked on macroeconomic theory and the lack of a pricing anchor in an economy with advanced financial markets when he was at Goldman Sachs, or when Hal Varian worked on search algorithms while at Google, they were doing seminal research but little of it led to journal article publication. Similarly, much of the work by economists at YahooResearch doesn't get published. But that work influences ideas, real-world policies, and discussions within economics.

My fifth objection to any journal article metric is that it is highly discriminatory against what I call "hands-on" research—research done to directly contribute to a policy debate on a problem. In my view, this is the most appropriate type of research for the majority of economics researchers. By that I mean that most researchers should not be trying to do cutting-edge scientific research and hands-off applied policy research. A well-functioning economics profession only needs a percentage of researchers doing such research—perhaps 5 percent of the current profession. Since the composition of that 5 percent is unknown, if four times that percentage—20 percent—of the profession focuses their primary energy on such research the probability of someone not doing it who should be doing it is exceedingly small. That leaves 80 percent of the economics profession who should not be devoting their primary research focus to it because they don't have the rigorous training, the intellectual firepower, or the inclination to do such cutting-edge theoretical or hands-off applied policy research.

I am not denigrating this 80 percent—I consider myself part of that 80 percent. We are often extremely bright and highly insightful. But true cutting-edge research requires a singularity of focus that borders on the obsessive. It requires enormous dedication often to the exclusion of important other aspects of life. The majority of us economists don't fit that bill. We are more well-rounded and more reasonable. We are (or at least we should be) more interested in, and capable of, using, teaching and marketing knowledge produced by economic scientists than we are in producing it.

Thus, my argument is that in a balanced profession, the large majority of the economics profession will not be focused on doing hands-off applied policy and cutting-edge scientific research. They will provide society with much more value-added if they focus their energies on teaching-oriented research and hands-on applied policy research that more directly relates to the type of work that the majority of their students will do.[7]

My most intense complaint with the current teaching of graduate economics in the United States is that that teaching is not directed at teaching graduate students to do hands-on research, because it is not taught by professors who do such hands-on research. Instead, graduate economics education in the US is designed to teach students to do hands-off research, even though the likelihood of their making a major contribution to such research is miniscule. In fact, to many economists, hands-off research is the only type of research that there is; they don't even consider hands-on research as research.

Hands-off policy analysis is written for other economists or advisors to policy-makers more than it is written for policy-makers themselves. It is what is most closely measured by a field-specific journal article metric such as is being advocated by top European economists. By design, hands-off research is not meant to guide policy-makers directly. To the degree that hands-off research actually comes to policy conclusions (generally it concludes with a call for more research), those conclusions are highly contingent on the implicit value judgments and goals in the models. *If* the policy-maker accepts these value judgments and goals, and *if* the world works like the model, then the policy recommendations of the hands-off research are relevant to policy-makers, but the hands-off research papers have no discussion of these issues, which makes the research of little direct value to the policy-maker. Hands-off researchers generally must leave it to an intermediary between the economic scientist and the policy-maker to do the translation.

Hands-on policy research is different from the policy research done by hands-off applied economists. Hands-on applied policy is written for policy-makers, not for other economists. Because it is written for policy-makers, any highly econometrically sophisticated analysis is put in a footnote. The emphasis is not on statistical precision, but on persuasiveness. The hands-on researcher is more concerned with making a convincing argument than with presenting a technically or econometrically sophisticated argument. Whereas hands-off applied policy is meant to be a contribution to the scientific debate, hands-on policy research is designed to contribute more directly to the policy debates in a country. Whereas hands-off policy analysis concentrates on the scientific aspect of policy, hands-on policy analysis applies scientific knowledge to policy by integrating economic knowledge and economic models into a broader framework.

This distinction between hands-on and hands-off applied policy research is especially important for a consideration of European graduate economics programs because traditional European programs have given students training in both hands-on and hands-off policy analysis. They have done so by emphasizing more history of thought, more intuition, and more discussion of context in their training than is currently done. In the past, professors at traditional European programs could do more hands-on applied policy research, and could teach a broader approach to economic reasoning than they can now, precisely because their research output was not subject to a quantitative measurement that gives no weight to such research output. (They may not have done enough of it because they did not have strong enough incentives to do any type of research, but they did more of it than they will in a system using a metric that gives zero weight to such research.)

Based on the US experience, that broader approach to teaching and that focus on training to do hands-on research, which has characterized traditional European graduate economics programs, is unlikely to continue into the future. All those aspects of economists' training have been culled from US programs, and are in the process of being culled from the global economics programs where I interviewed students. The reason is that such broad training is not helpful in training people in the hands-off policy analysis that has a reasonable outlet in the journals. That's one of the characteristics that differentiated the Oxford program from the other programs. Because Oxford was less concerned about preparing students to write journal articles, it provided a better training for students to do hands-off research. Consider an Oxford student's comment in response to a question about what the Oxford program is making out of its students:

> I'd say that they are producing economists. I know that sounds vacuous, but in fact, it suggests that their mindset is very general. That means that if you want to be an academic economist, a policy-maker, or go to work for an investment bank, that's fine. This is consistent with the general Oxford ethos—you read what you want, you learn what you want, and we'll push you in economics, but beyond that I think they really are agnostic as to what we do. (p. 119)

That is precisely the sense that I believe that the ideal graduate program designed to teach both hands-on and hands-off economic researchers would have.

The appropriate metric for hands-on policy research is its effect on policy, not its publication in an economics journal, especially journal articles written for other economists. It might involve writing an economics position paper for a political candidate, or it might involve developing a more efficient method for non-profit hospitals to process patients.[8] Hands-on research is written for actual decision-makers and its output is useful advice to those decision-makers. It is not written for other economists.

True hands-on research is often highly time-dependent. A "better" answer provided later than some pre-specified time is often useless. With the adoption of a journal article metric, such hands-on research output, which may well be the most important research output of economists, is discouraged. Hence my conclusion: *unless the metrics are adjusted to include this hands-on applied research, one of the major strengths of traditional European programs in training students to do such research will be undermined.*

Hands-off and hands-on researchers are, of course, related. Some of the best hands-off research is done by hands-on researchers who are able to stand back from their hands-on research and draw broader lessons and generalizations from that hands-on research. Researchers who can do it all should be classified as international treasures; they should be treated as such. Similarly, to do good hands-on research requires a knowledge of relevant hands-off research. Thus, I am not arguing for a total separation. I am simply arguing for a differentiation and an acceptance that both are important and that both get respect.

When the two types of research are both respected, and integrated, they complement each other. The problem develops when the two are separated, so that hands-off research is done by researchers with little knowledge or awareness of what is occurring on the ground in hands-on research, or when hands-on researchers are unaware of the advances that hands-off researchers are making. The current US system encourages that separation. In my view, both types of researchers need to know what the others are doing, but *they don't need to be able to do it.* They need a consumer's knowledge of the other activity, not a producer's knowledge. It follows that graduate schools should be providing the majority of students with a consumer's knowledge of scientific theory. In the US they aren't doing that, and aren't even trying to do that. They are only trying to train students to produce knowledge. The result is numerous students graduate with little sense of what the research objective is, and how it fits into the broader theoretical questions that scientific economists are trying to answer.

In settings where only hands-off research counts in the metric, as has happened in many US programs, the problem becomes cumulative. As students are recruited who are inclined towards hands-off rather than hands-on research, and as professors think only about hands-off research output, no one even recognizes that hands-on research is missing. Those individuals who are inclined to do hands-on applied research are driven from academic institutions and are replaced by researchers who do hands-off applied research. They then teach students to do hands-off applied research, even though almost all the students' primary job will be in doing hands-on applied research. The result is that students' training becomes further and further removed from what the majority of those students will actually be doing, and eventually the expertise in doing hands-on applied research is lost. That, in my view, is what has happened in the United States, and it is the system that Europe is importing when it designs its program to mimic US programs.

I do not believe that all the profession should be teaching hands-on research; hands-off research is important for what might be called economists' economists. As I stated above, in my view about 20 percent of the profession devoted to such research is more than enough. That 20 percent should get enormous support. But, in my view, they are not the majority of the profession, and their needs in training should not drive the training and measurement of output for the other 80 percent, as is now the case in US programs.

HOW TOP US PROGRAMS AVOID THE PROBLEMS CAUSED BY THE RANKINGS

The top US programs have avoided the worst of the problems caused by journal article metrics by not taking the metrics too seriously. The better the school, the less seriously metrics are taken. Although the economics ranking sub-industry developed in the United States in the 1970s, the journal article metrics that it created were not given significant prominence in funding or research, and top US economists and economics programs paid little attention to it. The rankings attracted most interest among non-top-tier programs that wanted to build their programs up to top tier, and thought they could do it by hiring and promoting people who scored highly in the rankings. Thus, over time, the formal rankings of programs, and of economists, became used in US economics programs for promotion decisions, especially at second-tier programs.[9] Most top economists that I talk to still do not take these rankings too seriously; they make their own decisions about who is a good economist and which is a good program. The rankings are certainly not something that the American

Economic Association even implicitly endorses in the way that the European Economic Association has done in its journals.[10]

Given this dismissive attitude by top US economists, I was surprised by the strong reliance on quantitative metrics of quality-weighted journal article output that seemed to characterize my discussions with top global European economists, and with the current reforms in European economics. In my mind that concern and focus are misplaced, both because the quantitative measures being used don't measure full output of economists, and because they don't provide a meaningful measure of future innovative cutting-edge research output, which is the type of research that can move programs into the top globally-ranked set of programs in the long run. A focus on journal article output metrics reflects a short-run, mimic-the-stars mentality that is the hallmark of second-tier programs.

As in the United States, in Europe the problem of overemphasis on journal article metrics tends to be less at higher-rank programs. A quantitative metric emphasizing journal article publications is both more relevant there (because top programs can reasonably focus on making global contributions to economic science) and less used there (because the economists there know that research contribution cannot be measured in a strict quantitative measure, and only use it as a very rough guide—which is how a quantitative measure is best used). My concern is, therefore, less with those top European global programs where their graduates have a reasonable chance of going on to teach in other top global programs, and more with those programs whose graduates do not have a reasonable chance to get a job teaching at other top programs, but instead are much more likely to get jobs at teaching-oriented universities, or with government or EU ministry positions, where hands-on research is most important. These programs make up the majority of European graduate programs in economics.

The introduction of a strict journal article metric for measuring output is of most concern for traditional European programs that do not have the option that US programs do: not taking the metrics too seriously. The lack of that option for European schools is an important reason why I oppose using the metrics in Europe. The reason is that European traditional academic institutions are different from most US academic institutions. European traditional universities are state-funded to a much greater degree than is the case in the United States. US private universities and even US state-funded universities face far fewer government directives about their internal decisions than is the case in Europe. In the United States the closest academic institutions we have to traditional European programs are unionized US academic institutions. Thus, one should use US unionized academic institutions as a guide to what will likely happen to European programs if a journal article metric is widely adopted.

Because of the need for "certifiable fairness" in contract negotiations in universities where unions exist, the programs' and universities' discretion about hiring and firing is significantly reduced, and metrics that are loose guidelines in other US schools have become rigid metrics in programs at unionized universities. Unionized programs have carefully classified lists of what counts (and how much it counts) for tenure and promotion decisions. They read like a Chinese menu. These lists, which can become 40 or 50 pages long, and can include weighting factors for the number of words on a page among hundreds of other dimensions, lead to a research corollary to Gresham's Law—at a program that relies strictly on a formal metric of research output, pedestrian research drives out creative and novel research. The reason is that, faced with such a list, rational researchers who are close to the minimum choose to publish in the "least costly" venue (the journals that require the least work for the highest measured gain in the metric) to them; they structure their research agenda accordingly. Researchers who are far above the minimum go elsewhere. It is not by chance that none of the top 20 economics programs in the United States are in unionized universities.

The unionized US program example suggests that if European economics is successful in establishing a strict journal article research metric, the result will be stultifying to much of the novel work that is currently taking place in Europe. It will create a static and pedestrian research environment rather than an environment that serves as the incubator for novel ideas, which the current European environment allows. (See Rosser et al., 2010, for a further discussion of this argument.) Researchers looking into long-range issues, advanced speculative work, or researchers setting off in new directions would be selected out of the European economics profession and replaced by "game playing" researchers who are more focused on maximizing output as measured by the metric. In my view, the strict adoption of such a metric will turn the majority of top traditional European universities into a set of perpetual second-tier global programs, similar in character to the perpetual second-tier US programs, rather than turning top European programs into serious competitors for dominance of global economics.[11]

THE NEED FOR CHANGE IN EUROPEAN PROGRAMS

I have argued at length with many top European economists about these issues, and most of them fully recognize the problems with formal quantitative rankings. They defend their support of such metrics for traditional

European economics programs by arguing that the need to change the institutional structure of traditional European programs is so great that it is worth the costs the rankings would impose. Their goal is to make European economics competitive with US economics, and they feel that the lack of pressure to do research in traditional European programs makes that impossible. They argue that introducing quantitative measures of research, and basing funding on those admittedly imperfect measures, would increase the pressure to do quality research and should be implemented.

Alan Kirman, Professor of Economics at Toulouse, a leading progressive figure in European economics, and a highly respected creative scientific researcher, captured what I call the progressive view when he stated:

> So my objection to these guys is that early on in their lives they get tenure, and they get a position for life at 29 or 30. This guy is called teacher and researcher— I just have the feeling that the guys should be doing something other than 6 hours of teaching a week. I think that's the killer in the French system. All universities are supposed to be the same, so everyone has the same job. You don't have some universities that are research oriented, and others that are teaching oriented, and we should have. It should match the students with the universities to best serve their needs. (Kirman, in Rosser et al., 2010, forthcoming)

Many other top economists I spoke with were a bit more politically correct in their statements, but their views were the same. The feeling of top European economics researchers is that traditional European economics needs to be shaken up if it is going to have a chance of competing globally with the United States, and they are willing to bear the costs that introducing an imperfect journal article metric will impose.[12]

MAKING RESEARCH PAY ITS OWN WAY: USING THE MARKET TO GUIDE RESEARCH

Just about all European economists that I speak with, whether they favor journal article metrics or not, believe that there are serious problems with the incentive structure of traditional European universities. The system was designed for a different era when there were far fewer professors and university students. That system only had researchers that the system had chosen as top, and they could reasonably be given enormous freedom. The entire professorate fit into the 20 percent that I now am suggesting should be focused on such research. Today, because of the expansion of the university system, that is no longer the case. As universities have changed their mission from teaching a small elite to teaching a much larger percentage of the population, the institutional structure of the universities has not changed. So I agree; change is needed. But much more change than could be accomplished by a change in the output metric used to judge research is needed.

HOW TO REALLY SHAKE UP EUROPEAN ECONOMICS: A MARKET-BASED RESEARCH SOLUTION

Were the introduction of a journal article metric the only way to introduce change into the European academic economics research community, I might be persuaded by the argument that the metrics are needed to shake up the European system. But it isn't, and in this section, I outline an alternative way of introducing change into the European academic system, which I call the market-based research solution. I suspect that this proposal will sound radical, but for economists it should not be seen as radical. It should be seen simply as the application of economic reasoning to academic institutional design. As I will show, the market-based research solution achieves precisely what proponents of change want— stronger incentives for research. But it does so in a way that avoids the biases and problems of a rigid journal output metric that is now being introduced.

The essence of the proposal is to make the research pay of the professor dependent on the professor meeting a market-determined metric rather than a journal article research metric. The proposal would involve the establishment of a market mechanism that eliminates the need for a system-wide post-research formal output metric because it builds an output metric into the funding mechanism for that research, just as a market does. To be honest, the proposal doesn't eliminate the need for a metric nor the need to judge a researcher's output. Instead it pushes the problem of judging output to the funders of the research since they are the ultimate demanders—the ones providing the funding for the research. The market mechanism is designed to reveal their demand for research. They may, and in the case to top scientific researchers I will argue, should, transfer the problem of judging research back to academics and to the university community. I strongly believe that scientific researchers should have freedom and flexibility to conduct their research. But that transfer of authority about judging research from the funding agency will be an explicit choice of the funding agencies, not a default option as it is now, in which researchers take funding given to professors for teaching and use it to fund research activities.

Specifically, the proposal would establish research vouchers, which I will call ERUs (European Research Units), measured in euros. Funding agencies will distribute these ERUs either directly or indirectly to the demanders of economics research in an amount equal to the research funding for salaries that it is providing the university. In turn, the demanders of research would transfer these ERUs to professors upon completion of a research project they choose to fund, or that they want or need done. Why will the researcher want these ERUs? Because his or her pay for research (which will likely consists of about 50 percent of his or her total pay) will depend on the professor accumulating ERUs of that amount.

The research projects funded by these ERUs could be developed by the professor, or by the funding agency. The professor would then pass on the ERUs to the university as the measure of his or her research output, which would satisfy the funding agency that the research is completed. This market, I claim, will direct professors' research much more efficiently than any introduction of a research output metric.

The market-based research solution is relatively simple—it modifies the funding system of universities, so that that funding system directly incorporates an incentive to do research. If a professor does research he or she gets paid for the research portion of his or her salary; if he or she doesn't do research he or she doesn't get paid for the research portion of his or her salary. In that way the market-based research system provides a "market" answer to the incentive problem that is both more and less radical than the "impose a quantitative metric" answer that is currently being implemented.[13]

THE PROBLEM THE PROPOSAL IS MEANT TO SOLVE

Since the proposal is rather novel, let me start by summarizing the problem that it is meant to solve—instilling in university professors a strong incentive to do *useful* research.[14] The reason such an incentive is necessary is that, while university professors are paid to teach and to do research, neither activity can be easily quantified, which means that professors have to be given a fair amount of discretion to choose their research topics and to choose what they teach. Because of that necessary discretion, in the current institutional environment in traditional European universities, a professor's pay does not depend closely on his or her research. This leads to an incentive problem.

The sense I get from many top European economics researchers is that they believe that too many traditional European professors are taking advantage of that discretion and are not doing research. These top economics researchers argue that traditional European professors' failure to measure up in the journal article metric is proof that they are taking advantage of that discretion, and not working on research. Not everyone agrees with that assessment. The sense I get from many professors in traditional European programs is that the top economics researchers' assessment is incorrect; professors at many traditional programs believe that top researchers are simply not valuing the type of research that professors at traditional programs are doing. I am in no position to judge which of these views is more accurate, and one of the advantages of the system I am proposing is that it does not require any judgment on this question. Instead, it creates incentives for all professors to do research, but it allows for a much wider range of research than the quantitative journal article metrics allow.

SOME SPECIFICS OF THE PROPOSAL

Let me now discuss some specifics of the proposal. In this market-based research solution, the funding agencies for the university, such as the national governments, the European Union, and the local governments, would indirectly fund that portion of a professor's salary that is to be devoted to research by providing ERUs equal to the amount of salary funding that the funding agency provides the university to groups or agencies that have a demand for the professor's research. The funding agency would institute a rule that the university will get the funding only for the research portion of a professor's pay when the university provides it with the ERUs that the funding agency has passed out.

In turn, the professor will only get paid for the research portion of his or her salary when he or she provides certification to the university that the research is done by providing the ERUs to the university. (In practice, I would expect that initially the funding agencies would advance the payments to the universities, and universities would advance payments to professors, with the certification coming later, but that is a technicality.) The important point is that payment for the research would be contingent on the research that the funding agency wants done is done. No research, no payment to the university; and no payment to the university, no pay to the faculty member. Since the ERUs will be provided to the professor by the demanders of the research, the transfer of those ERUs to the professor and university will provide a certification that the research the demanders are subsidizing is done.

It should be obvious to the reader that the funding agencies' role in guiding research would be significantly increased in this proposal. They would guide research by their choice of to whom to give the ERUs. Those funding agencies that wanted to fund scientific hands-off research would provide the ERUs to scientific foundations whose role would be significantly increased under this system. These scientific foundations would not only provide funding for supplemental research funds as they often do now; they would also provide standard salary funding for the research component of a professor's work. Thus, any funded scientific hands-off research that is subsidized will have to make it through an initial scientific peer review panel that will decide that the research is worthwhile research. This places an initial hurdle in the path of scientific research. Successful negotiation of this hurdle is likely to significantly increase the possible usefulness of the research.

My strong suspicion is that when they are presented with the "academic research question" in this manner, many funding agencies would not choose to fund as much scientific hands-off research as this proposal would bring about. Instead, they would choose to fund more hands-on research. They would do this by providing their ERUs not to scientific agencies to fund hands-off scientific research, but instead to applied policy non-profit agencies, NGOs, national government agencies, and local government agencies. These agencies, in turn, would distribute ERUs to local non-profits that would either develop research questions that they need answered, that these agencies need done, or develop mechanisms that would judge grant proposals that the applied policy funding agencies find useful. Thus, these agencies could either use their ERUs to commission research for themselves, or they could distribute the ERUs to other agencies, such as the university itself, to commission research. A professor's research agenda would then include in it a plan to acquire sufficient ERUs to cover that part of his or her salary that is supposed to be devoted to research.[15]

While this proposal sounds like a major change in the research funding system, it need not be. By that I mean that the present system of funding research could be mimicked by this market system. To do that the funding agencies would allocate all their ERUs to universities, which in turn would allocate them to professors. This will leave the professor as both the supplier and demander of research, which is precisely the position professors are in now. They demand research, and they supply it themselves. Were funding agencies and universities to follow that allocation method, the ERU solution would simply make more explicit the current internal university funding method for research process.

Thinking of the research problem of universities within this framework highlights why the current system is not working, and the reason why European universities are trying to restructure. The current system makes the demander of research also the supplier of research. This combining of the demander and supplier roles in research can work in highly controlled environments in which either one can be confident that the researchers have a strong inherent desire to do top research. The current reforms are attempting to add the careful measurement of output to a system that allows professors to choose their own research. My proposal is to separate out the demanders of research from the suppliers, and thereby provide some market guidance for research.

FUNDING HANDS-OFF SCIENTIFIC RESEARCH

My suspicion is that, while the existing funding agencies could design the market-based research solution to operate in the same way that the current system does, they will not do so. They will, instead, allocate some portion of these ERUs to outside funding agencies such as the European Science Foundation, whose budget would probably increase substantially, because it would include not only supplemental research funds, but also a much larger degree of salary support than currently is the case. This would add more competition into the funding process. In order to get their ERUs necessary for research funding, professors will have to submit competitive proposals to the European Science Foundation and other scientific funding agencies and have the proposals judged by peer review to be "good science" at the proposal stage. I would also suspect that there would be a large increase in the number of scientific research funding agencies, which would each likely focus on a different type of scientific economics research.

An important aspect of this proposal is that it makes clear that research funding for professors need not be just for scientific research. As I discussed above, in my view, about 20 percent of economists' research devoted to such work should be more than sufficient. That 20 percent funding would give a high probability that any proposal that has substantial scientific possibilities would be funded.

Some of this scientific funding will go through the European Science Foundation, but other aspects of it will go through national and local governmental units, collections of universities, and or specific universities, which I expect would set up research demand agencies to oversee the research. Thus, my vision is that there would be a number of competing European, national, and local scientific research foundations that would be established to allocate these ERUs to scientific research faculty in a similar fashion to what the European Science Foundation does now. Thus, there would be multiple funding agencies, each with its own vision of what "good" scientific research is. Academic researchers would then put in their proposals, and if the applicants are successful, they are paid the ERUs that were specified as salary payment in the proposal.

I would expect another 25 percent of the research funding to be for what I call teaching-oriented research. Teaching-oriented research is not scientific research, but is research that would benefit teaching. Work in economic history, the history of economic thought, institutional economics involving case studies, general policy work, and work involving discussions of broader ideas within economics all falls within this category. This research is not science, but it enriches teaching, and one would want teaching-oriented professors to do this type of research. Thus, I would see funders establishing teaching foundations that would be given ERUs to allocate through a competitive process in the same way that the scientific foundations allocate their ERUs. There is much of this teaching-oriented research already going on in Europe although it is being squeezed out by the focus on a quality-weighted journal article research metric. This proposal would provide a channel for it to get funding if the funding agencies believe that it has merit.

I would expect that the research funding units would not only have an initial peer review of the proposal but possibly also a peer review at the finish of the research, to see if the project met its stated goals.[16] That post-research peer review is essentially what is now done in the journal publication process, and this post-research peer review process could still be done through existing journals, so that when journals accept a paper, it is assumed to meet the peer review standard. However, such a journal article procedure is costly and highly inefficient. Given the enormous expansion of the Internet it would be far more efficient for research funding agencies, or universities, to create a separate peer review "publication" system that totally bypasses existing journals. In this alternative post-research peer review process, the funding agencies would essentially perform the function of current journals. They would post all their funded research on their website, making it available to all researchers without cost.

How could they fund this online publication? With ERUs. Thus, my proposal recognizes that peer review is an important research activity—one that currently gets significantly undervalued. (If the funding agencies chose to do the post-research peer review through existing journals, they could transfer sufficient ERUs to journals to pay reviewers for their work.) Thus, I would expect that the funding for each project would include a certain percentage of funding for both initial peer reviews that would be necessary to decide what proposals to fund, and post-research peer review—reviews of whether the research achieved its ends. Instead of waiting for all discussion and interaction about research until after the research is finished and submitted to a journal, more of the peer review would move up to the proposal stage, where the suggestions of reviewers can more easily be incorporated into the analysis. Thus, this proposal incorporates a greater amount of peer review into the process, and funds the peer review process. In fact, I would expect that a few researchers could earn all their ERUs by reviewing articles for the funding agency.[17]

If this research posting and post-research peer review is done, my suspicion is that the change in funding methods will significantly reduce the demand for academic journals, since the research will be available on the funding agency's designated website and since publication in a journal would be far less important to researchers than it is now. Researchers' primary concern will be in satisfying the granting agency that they have done a good job, since when they go back at another time with a proposal, the agency will look at how well the researcher did the previous time.

Eventually, I would argue, this system would, and should, replace journal articles as the method through which research is "published." This replacement is not as large a change as it may seem because, in practice, print journals have already been superseded by working papers as the primary vehicle by which research findings are conveyed among active researchers. Journals serve more as a means to transmit information to less active researchers and stand as a tombstone, marking a researcher's property rights on the ideas in the research. The elimination of journals would free up time that currently goes into editing and reviewing for journals—time that would be transferred into peer reviewing proposals and provide invited comments on finished research.

For top academic researchers, I would expect that there would be little change in the system. I would expect that top researchers (say, the top 20 percent of European professors), who have shown themselves to be highly productive in the past either in scientific research or in teaching-oriented research, would be given blanket multi-year research grants—say, five years of research on the topics of their choice—by research funding agencies. Some of the most productive researchers could be considered "European research treasures" and be given a lifetime research grant. Thus, this group of top research professors would find little difference between the new system and the current system. In fact, there is a strong likelihood that under my proposed system, they would be given even more support for, and flexibility in, research than they have now.

The proposal will have a much larger impact on less productive researchers. If professors are not successful in meeting their ERU research requirements, then their university salaries would be only for teaching and service, not for research. It is possible that if they wanted to make up for the missing research units, the university might allow them temporarily to make them up in additional teaching, but I would advocate that only as a temporary measure. I take this position because I believe that to be a good teacher one should be doing research that directly relates to the type of work that one's students will be going into.

Thus, if a professor continues to be unsuccessful in meeting his or her ERU requirements, then he or she would lose his or her positions as a combined research/teaching professor, and will either have to take a teaching-only position or find another job. The general incentives for research that such a proposal would instill would be considerably greater than they are in the current system, or that would exist in a system that imposed a journal publication metric.

While this proposal is radical in the sense that it changes research funding decisions, and gives funding agencies much more control over the type of research that professors do, it preserves the advantages of the traditional European system much better than does the adoption of a journal article metric. Because they are meeting their ERU requirement, those researchers who are successful in the proposed generalized grant system will have much more flexibility about what research to do, and whether and where to "publish" it. Thus, for top researchers, this system will be more like the traditional European system that gave researchers significant freedom, letting them "do their thing." They would worry less about publishing and more about *thoughtful research* over *publishable research*.

WHAT FUNDING MEETS THE MARKET TEST?

I don't know what decisions the funding agencies will make about how much of various types of research to fund. Initially, I suspect that they would likely focus on the same type of research that is currently done. However, as funding agencies gain experience they will see the value of different types of research, and I would expect that the type of research being funded would change. That is the beauty of the market. It directs funds to where there is a demand. The current system doesn't do that. Under this ERU funding system, funding agencies will reveal their preferences about what research they want to see done and by whom, by giving their ERUs to groups that do the type of research they want done.

If they give all their ERUs to agencies such as the European Science Foundation, the funding agencies will create a large increase in the academic journal article type of research that the top quality-weighted journals focus on now. If they give all the research vouchers to teaching-oriented research foundations, one would see an increase in economic history, institutional economics, and history of economic thought research. But if you notice, in my discussion I suggested that only 50 percent of the current funding would go to these types of research. That reflects my belief that 50 percent of researchers' time will be the type of research that the funding agencies will choose to fund. What I am suggesting is that when faced with the true cost of hands-off research in economics, funding agencies will decide that 50 percent of the resources that are currently devoted to hands-off economic research is not worth the costs.[18]

I base this expectation on the fact that there is little to no demand for the hands-off research among anyone other than other academic institutions. Academic libraries have become the primary demanders of academic economics research, and they pay enormous prices for some of the journals that publish it. That high price, however, is not for the research; it is only for the cost of peer reviewing and transmitting and packaging the information by the journals—information could be (and often has been) transmitted to most researchers at much lower cost when it is posted on the Internet as part of a working paper series. The reality of the current research funding system is that universities subsidize the production of research for which there is no revealed demand other than by the same universities that subsidize its production.

The largest subsidy that universities provide—the subsidy for actually doing the research—is hidden by the current funding system. So the nature of the current system is that the university (and thus indirectly the funding agencies of the universities) provides a large subsidy to current research on both the supply side and the demand side. Universities are paying their professors to do research, and then university libraries are paying publishers for transmitting that research back to the researchers who are doing it—researchers who could have had easy access to it anyway were the research just posted on the web. That is hardly the type of situation that gives one a reassurance that the research that is currently being conducted is beneficial.

Consider the cost of the research embodied in a typical issue of an economics journal. For sake of argument let's say that an article takes 200 hours to write, and that we can value the researcher's time at $100 per hour.[19] That means that the research cost $20 000 in the researcher's time. Let's also say that the process of reviewing the article has taken ten hours, which valued at $100 per hour adds another $1000, so let us say that the cost of the typical academic journal article in terms of time is $21 000. To that must be added the cost of actually typesetting and distributing the article, for which I will add another $1000 per article. That means that an issue of an academic journal with 15 articles in it has about $320 000 worth of "research" in it. The question that the funding agencies would have to pose under this ERU system is whether it, as representative of society, would be willing to pay $320 000 for that information in that journal.

My suspicion is that much of the current hands-off research published in economics cannot meet that market test. I agree with one of the students I interviewed in his assessment of the current hands-off research when he stated, "In a top journal like the *Quarterly Journal of Economics* I'd say at least half [of the articles published] are useless. Probably 20 percent are useful and the rest are unclear. . ... Fifty percent will never be cited or read again" (Colander, 2007). This student's view is not an outlier; many of the economists I speak with would agree with it.

WHAT RESEARCH IS WORTHWHILE?

The fact that much of the current research would not meet a market test does not mean that economists are not capable of doing research that can meet a market test. There is a large demand for economists' "research" as demonstrated by the large number of economic consultancies. My suspicion is that there are large areas where hands-on research would easily meet the market test. That is why I left 50 percent of the research funding to go to hands-on research. My belief is that when funding agencies are faced with the full cost of research, many of them will decide that *they want to fund research that is fundamentally different than the type of research currently being done by academic economists.* Specifically, I suspect that many funding agencies would want to encourage much more hands-on research, in which researchers use their expertise to solve particular problems or assist local non-profit groups in solving a community problem.[20]

Currently, such hands-on research gets little emphasis by US academics since it is not counted in economists' output. My understanding is that traditional European economists do more of this type of research, but that it is being discouraged by the introduction of the journal article metric. This proposal allows it to be counted, and thus is much more consistent with the way traditional European programs operate than is the journal article metric.

Here is what I would expect to happen to research funding were this proposal adopted. Some funding agencies would not give all their ERUs for scientific or teaching-oriented research, but instead give their ERUs to state or local governments to distribute. These in turn would give their ERUs to non-profit and governmental agencies who need actual economic questions answered and problems solved. The agencies would post these "research jobs" on a website devoted to matching the demand for research with researchers. They could either post the number of ERUs they have to pay for the research or they could put the research out for bid, but ultimately an agreement would be made. The research could be for general consulting, or for a specific project, such as setting up a study or simply reviewing a study that has already been done. Agencies given ERUs would be required to post performance evaluations with the funding agencies. These would serve as post-performance evaluations; they could be published on the website, or simply provided to other agencies that are choosing with whom to contract in the future.

IMPLEMENTING THE RESEARCH FUNDING PLAN

The market research funding plan is a radical change from the current system, and if it had to be implemented all at once, it probably would never be implemented at all. But it does not have to be implemented all at once. It can be phased in gradually, with initially, say, 5 percent of professors' research pay contingent on their getting ERUs, and then, if the plan works, increasing that by a certain percentage per year. Alternatively, it could be introduced for a sub-set of universities that are most likely to focus on hands-on research.

I recognize that if the plan had to be implemented by universities, it would likely never be implemented. It places much more pressure on professors to do research than they would like, and much more outside review of university research than many universities would like. What makes the plan feasible is that it is not dependent on university implementation; the funding agencies are the ones with the power to unilaterally implement it. For most European universities, this means that the plan can be implemented by various levels of government. Outside foundations could also provide their funding to universities in this manner, essentially offering funding to universities who agree to accept the ERUs from their faculty as evidence of successful hands-on research.[21] By choosing this route, foundations could provide both the university and a non-profit agency with support under the same funding proposal.

FEEDBACK FROM THE RESEARCH TO THE TRAINING OF ECONOMISTS

The above discussion of an alternative research funding method has moved considerably away from the training of economists that the survey and interviews discussed in earlier chapters focused on. But I see the two as directly related. Professors are best at training students to be like themselves—professors train students to do the type of research that they themselves do. My problem with the US graduate economics education system that Europe seems to be trying to mimic is that it is far too uniform.

Almost all US graduate economics students are being trained to be scientific researchers even though most of them have a very low probability of doing serious scientific research. The system trains students to be efficient journal article writers regardless of the value to society of another journal article. Most graduate students in economics will make their contribution to society through their teaching and their hands-on research. Almost all graduate students' students will only be doing hands-on research. But the graduate students, and hence their students, are being trained to do hands-off research. That, to me, is the central problem with global graduate economics education today. It is one that the Americanization of European economics is making worse.

The tensions that are created between preparing students for one type of work when they will actually be doing another show up in my interviews with the students. Consider some of the students' comments for the interviews in earlier chapters:

- I got no intuition at all in the core courses micro, macro, or econometrics; it was all math. It was not difficult, but it was just math. It was different in the field courses. At least that's what I remember.
- You don't need a broad knowledge of economics institutions in the economy to succeed as an economist, which to some extent is really bad. You don't have to follow the public debate in any subject. Maybe this is good science but I'm not sure. The environment attracts people who are not really interested in the public debate, or policy. I definitely agree. For me it is also a problem since my goal is not teaching. I don't want to become a professor.
- Another difference between Europe and the United States is that the academic tradition here in Europe is more open to a wider-ranging discussion, more radical viewpoints. It is not a problem taking courses in, say, classical economics. European universities are more connected to the world. You can get that in many schools in Europe although not in this particular school because this program is very US-style. I think that the historical perspective on economics is not part of the US-style program. Here in Europe it has been part of the program but is being abandoned.
- What they ask from you is mostly mathematical skills. There is little intuition.
- It's not really connected to policy issues.
- My first macro class here was on growth theory; I had done my undergraduate thesis on growth theory, so I expected to know something about it. I didn't. The professor walked in and wrote a Hamiltonian on the board. It was a bit shocking. In macro, you get no clue

about policy. Any clue that I got, I got later studying by myself. In micro, that's not true. In micro, we did a lot of game theory; that was fantastic—mechanism design. The general equilibrium studies were a mess; there was no intuition. I remember this hyperplane that separates everything from everything. You just memorize. If you had time to study it, it might have been better. Econometrics was just matrices. I remember that I could do everything with matrices; now I remember almost nothing. There was no practical econometrics in the core courses. In an upper-level econometrics course, we got more applied work.

The argument that there is a mismatch between the training and what the students will be working on is even stronger for undergraduate economics students. Almost no undergraduate students will ever go on to be scientific researchers. Instead, they will apply the economics they learn to real-world problems and to making decisions about what type of policies the government should follow. If their professors have not been taught to do that, those professors will not be especially good at teaching undergraduate students to do that. In my view, as a society, we get the connection between graduate work and undergraduate work backwards in the training of professors. In the current environment, undergraduate school is seen as a feeder for graduate school. Thus, the needs of graduate schools drive research and determine the content of what is taught. In my view it should be the reverse for the majority of professors whose primary contribution is teaching.

In thinking about the training of professors who will be primarily undergraduate teachers of economics, or hands-on researchers, the needs of undergraduate training and hands-on researchers should dominate. By that I mean that most graduate schools should be seen primarily as training future professors of undergraduates and hands-on researchers. Both these activities require a broad-based core that provides students with significant experience and expertise in hands-on research.

If the funding agencies agree with me that only about a fifth of the research in economics journals is a fundable contribution to scientific research, the market-based research solution would direct graduate economics education toward those ends. It will lead to the majority of professors doing much more teaching-related research and *applying* economic reasoning to problems, and to solving real-world problems than it currently does. It will funnel professional research activities toward direct involvement with the economy—writing position papers, showing how systems can be more efficiently organized, and doing empirical studies necessary to make decisions in real time.

FEASIBLE CHANGE

As I stated at the beginning of this book, I am a realist, and most people who read the above proposal will see me more as a wild-eyed dreamer. So, let me say now that I do not expect Europe to immediately adopt my research funding proposal. I present it more in the hope of stopping what I see as the worst type of change—making the European system into a second-rate copy of the US system and thereby incorporating all the problems that the US system has into the European system. What I want to encourage is change that builds on the strengths of the European system, which I see as its openness to different types of research, its diversity, and the greater freedom that it gives to incoming graduate students. Those are all attributes that are useful for training students to be undergraduate professors and hands-on researchers, but not especially useful for training students to be efficient journal-article writers. They are the strengths that the mimicking of the US graduate system, with its first-year focus on a theoretical core, will undermine. It is my belief that thinking about the problem of incentives and research in the framework of the market-based research funding system will help people to see the problems with that US system, so that even if they don't adopt the market-based research funding system, they will be less likely to adopt changes that undermine the current strengths of the European system.

CONCLUSION: SOME CAUTIONS

Towards that end, I will conclude this chapter with a brief discussion of some of the cautions that the analysis suggests for European graduate economics reform.

Maintain as Much Differentiation and Diversity as Possible

Instead of directing all researchers to do the same type of research, as the journal article metric does, the market-based research funding system encourages diversity in research. Faced with this funding system for research, I would expect that some universities would specialize in various types of research while others would include all types of research. For example, a few universities might decide to focus only on hands-off scientific research. They would hire primarily researchers who could win multi-year open scientific research grants. (They would likely have a different undergraduate program with professors whose interests are more towards teaching and hands-on research.) Other universities, especially those with large undergraduate teaching responsibilities, would decide to focus more on teaching-oriented research and hands-on research. They would primarily hire professors whose interest is in teaching and practical problem-solving. If European universities don't adopt the market-based research funding system, they should figure out some other way of encouraging that diversity in research.

Think of Economics Output and Training as Multi-dimensional

For those programs that attempt to train students in both hands-off research and hands-on research, the market-based funding system framework suggests that there should be multiple tracks with professors teaching students in the track that they will likely be going into. The best professor for hands-on research is likely to differ significantly from the best professor for hands-off research. The type of research that professors do largely determines the content of their courses that they teach. Teachers are best at teaching others to do what the teacher does. That means that teaching and research must mesh, and that the primary way to change teaching is to change research.

One of the reasons I put forward the "market-funded research" proposal is to change the research focus of some group of economics professors, and thereby change the training that students receive. Instead of training students in complicated theoretical issues and techniques, programs focusing on hands-on research will focus much more on training them in more practical types of research and skills. Far less time will go into preparing students to write scientific journal articles. This training in hands-on research, I argue, will be more appropriate to the large majority of graduate students, and to almost all undergraduate students. Thus, students would take a set of core courses together, and then specialize in hands-on research or hands-off research courses.

Teach Broad Ideas in the Core Relevant to all Types of Economists

For programs that do not specialize, but attempt to teach all types of students, compromises will have to be made in the training they offer. Specifically, the core courses will likely have to be jointly taught. I would strongly suggest that in making that compromise, the core be that part of economics that is most relevant to all three groups. In traditional European economics, students had enormous flexibility in their first couple of years of the PhD. They read and thought about issues. The new system being adopted follows the US system; it immediately immerses students into a highly technical core, and quickly pulls students up to speed technically.

If you are only interested in hands-off scientific research, the technical core approach to graduate economics education may make sense. But if my estimate of the demand for economics research is correct, then that type of research only involves one-fifth of the demand for research. So in creating such a technical core, you are discouraging students whose interests are more towards hands-on research and teaching undergraduates, and providing them with little training that is useful. To give the 20 percent the training that might be best for them, the 80 percent receive training that has little relevance for them. That, in my mind, is the height of inefficiency. It leads many of the students to drop out. A Pompeu Fabra student comment captured this problem. In response to a question of why so many students drop out he answered: "I think the students who find it different from what they expected are not happy. They feel cheated by economics." Another said: "There are a lot of complaints about the program among the students. They feel that they don't learn anything useful."

Still another says:

> The whole program has about 100 students with about 60–70 economics students. I would say that almost all of the economics students come with the intention to do a PhD. After one term many decide maybe not here, and maybe never. The finance program and management programs are different, because their Masters degrees have more market value than economics. (p. 81)

The traditional European system served the broader majority of students much better. It left those students who were so inclined to get the highly technical work later, and thus encouraged a broader set of students to stay in economics, which makes much more sense. Thus, from this perspective, European universities should carefully consider whether they want to change to a US-type of system, and if they do, they should reverse the core—putting more field courses that are relevant to all economists in the first year, and putting the highly technical courses as upper-level field courses for those interested in scientific economics.

Redesign the Exam System

While course content matters, the same course content can have quite different effects depending on the nature of the exam. One way to institute the diversity into the program is to use a variation of the Oxford outside examiner approach to grading exams. Oxford's use of outside examiners, and significant choice in which questions on the exam to answer, gives students much more flexibility in their studying. Who grades the exam is as important as what is taught. If European programs allow representatives of those institutions that are the primary demanders of their graduates to design and grade some of the questions on their exam, the courses would much more likely reflect what the students will be doing when they get out.

A Final Comment

Traditional European graduate economics programs need radical change. This chapter has argued that the current focus of that change—to get the universities to measure up in terms of a journal article metric—is not the way to go. It developed a proposal for radical change that better met the needs of European programs. I suspect the proposal is too radical for most. But even if one doesn't choose to adopt the radical change suggested, thinking of economics training within the framework of the research funding proposal should give one pause about making the type of changes that traditional European universities are beginning to make. The changes being made will essentially impose many of the worst elements of the US system rather than building on the strengths of the current European system.

In thinking about reform of European graduate economics, Dennis Mueller captured my view when he wrote that "what would be ideal would be to intensify competition within European academia without losing entirely, the broader, longer run perspective of the Europeans" (Mueller, 1995, p. 255). Whether that is possible remains to be seen, but it is my hope that this book will stimulate debate and further research on such questions.

NOTES

1. Each of these sub-elements of output can include many dimensions. The most ambiguous of these three is service, but it generally includes activities both within the economics profession and within the broader academic and societal community. Government, central bank, international government agency, business, and think tank economists have an even broader concept of output, and their output measure would significantly expand the areas that would fall under the service heading. Their service includes providing advice to policy-makers, weighing in on public and internal debates and policy issues by writing policy briefs, and talking with, and influencing, policy-makers and the general public.
2. The shortfall of European economists on the quality-weighted journal article metrics is noted in numerous articles.
3. I have developed this argument in Colander (2009).
4. In a recent paper Glenn Ellison (2007) has found that the journal peer review system is in decline at top US programs.
5. I have discussed these issues in Colander and Plum (2004).
6. ArXiv.org is the website where physicists post their working papers as a prelude to submission to journals; it is open source and permanently archived.
7. I develop this distinction further in Colander and Nopo (2008).

8.   Similarly, the appropriate output metric for a teacher would be writing a teaching article or a textbook.

9.   Top-tier programs tended to give far less weight to these rankings. In their view, good work leads to high rankings, not the other way around. The sense I get from economists at top programs is that if you have to think about rankings, then you probably don't have a truly top program. Few funding decisions in the United States are directly tied to these rankings although, informally, rankings are used to justify funding requests. Where faculty unions exist, these formal rankings have been highly formalized and embedded in formal promotion procedures. At most non-union schools, rankings of an economist's journal articles are just informally used, but they are nonetheless important.

10. In 1989, I reviewed much of the recent literature on ranking of US departments for the AEA's *Journal of Economic Perspectives*. In that article I expressed a view that was shared by the top economists I spoke with, and suggested that "the ranking game has been beat to death" (Colander, 1989, p. 141). I wrote: "Everyone knows that any ranking loses important dimensions and, among those active in the profession, the information about which schools rank where is known more precisely than the rankings disclose, especially in view of how quickly top individuals move from school to school and how quickly topics considered important change" (ibid.). Another recent survey of rankings in the United States came to a similar conclusion. It found that changes in ranking methods do not significantly change the top schools, but can significantly change at the medium- and lower-ranked schools (Thursby, 2000). Thursby writes, "There's not a hill of beans difference across large groups of departments" (p. 383).

11. For all the push by various non-top-tier US programs to improve in the rankings, there has been little shift over the years in the overall rankings of programs; no program has moved into the top group that was not close to the top group initially. One reason is that when a star or group of stars develops at lower-ranked programs, they are hired away by the higher-ranked, more prestigious, and generally wealthier, programs. A second reason is that competition at that level is extremely expensive; the top US schools have endowments in the multiple billions of dollars, and stand ready to hire away top researchers who develop elsewhere. Those programs that don't have enormous flexibility in hiring cannot compete in such a system.

12. This view is expressed by Portes (1987) and Drèze (2001), for instance.

13. The professors I have presented this proposal to have not been enthusiastic about it. This is not surprising. Few individuals like to submit themselves to the market, if they can receive the payment without submitting themselves to the market test.

14. I do not deal with the incentives for teaching in this book; that would require an entirely separate book.

15. There are many open variables in the plan that would have to be determined before it could be implemented. For example, pay could at times exceed the professor's standard salary if a professor undertakes significant research in a particular year. Generally, however, I would expect that in any year, researchers would not be paid more than their salary, so after they have done their required research, they would no longer have an economic incentive from the plan to do research, but they would be allowed to bank a certain amount of ERUs to give them freedom to do research that they want to do, for which they could not get funding in that particular year. Many, I suspect, would still do additional research, just as they do now without any economic incentive. To the degree that the research is considered valuable, it would increase their desirability to other schools, and thereby increase their potential income.

16. I would strongly encourage each funding unit to require all research funded by that agency to be posted on the funding unit's designated website, which would mean that it is accessible to all interested scholars. (The National Institute of Health in the United States has established such a requirement.)

17. If these changes occur, they would fundamentally alter the economics of for-profit journals, as reviewers would expect a payment for reviewing, which would eliminate the

subsidization. I would expect that this proposal would be highly disruptive to for-profit publishers. Non-profit publishers would be eligible for grants of ERUs from the funding agencies, and thus would be far less affected.

18. This does not mean it can't be done. If university professors want to do it, they can do it on their own time, just as anyone else can. Significant research is done on people's own time, and I suspect that unfunded research would continue to be done on professors' own time since many will likely do significantly more research than is necessary to acquire the ERUs they are required to earn to receive their "research pay."

19. This is a conservative estimate. On average, professors produce less than one article per year, which suggests that the time going into an article is significantly more than 200 hours if half the professor's time is supposed to go into research. Similarly, the $100 per hour is a low valuation if one compares it with economic consulting agencies where new economists working on a project are billed at $350 per hour, and top economists are often billed at $600 per hour. Were I to use these higher figures, the cost of an average article in research time is much more than $20 000.

20. One issue that I have avoided discussing here is private consulting and hands-on research. This could also count as research if the university is reimbursed the full cost for that percentage of the time that the researcher spends doing this private consulting. Thus, a hands-on researcher doing half-time consulting could fulfill his research requirement, but would be paid only that part of his or her salary that is for teaching.

21. This means that private universities, which get their financing through tuition, will not be required to implement the plan except to the degree that they are depending on outside funding. However, it would offer a way to implement state funding of research at private universities, since their professors could be allowed to compete for research funds just as do professors at state-funded universities. Thus, the plan could encourage the development of more private scientifically-oriented universities such as Bocconi.

References

Bewley, Truman (1999), *Why Wages Don't Fall During a Recession*, Cambridge, MA: Harvard University Press.

Cawley, John (2004), "A Guide (and Advice) for Economists on the U.S. Junior Academic Job Market", available at www.aeaweb.org/joe/articles/2004/cawley_2004.pdf (accessed 15 February 2009).

Colander, David (1989), "Research on the Economics Profession", *Journal of Economic Perspectives*, **3**(4), 137–48.

Colander, David (1998), "The Sounds of Silence: The Profession's Response to the COGEE Report", *American Journal of Agricultural Economics*, **80**(3), 600–607.

Colander, David (2006), "The Making of an Economist Redux", *Journal of Economic Perspectives*, **19**(1), 175–98.

Colander, David (2007), *The Making of an Economist Redux,* Princeton, NJ: Princeton University Press.

Colander, David (2008), "The Making of a Global European Economist", *Kyklos*, **61**(2), 215–36.

Colander, David (2009), "Can European Economics Compete with U.S. Economics? And Should It?", Middlebury College Working Paper No. 2009-IX.

Colander, David and Arjo Klamer (1987), "The Making of an Economist", *Journal of Economic Perspectives*, **1**(2), 95–111.

Colander, David and Hugo Nopo (2008), "The Making of a Global Latin American Economist", Middlebury College Working Paper, No. 2007-05.

Colander, David and Terry Plum (2004), "Efficiency, Journal Publishing and Scholarly Research", Middlebury College Department of Economics Working Paper No. 2004-19.

Drèze, Jacques (2001), "Economics and Universities in Europe", Mimeo, CORE, Louvain.

Ellison, Glenn (2007), "Is Peer Review in Decline?", NBER Working Paper No. 13272.

Frey, Bruno and Reiner Eichenberger (1992), "Economics and Economists: A European Perspective", *The American Economic Review*, **82**(2), May, 216–20.

Frey, Bruno and Reiner Eichenberger (1993), "American and European

Economics and Economists", *Journal of Economic Perspectives*, **7**(4), 185–93.

Frey, Bruno, Silke Humbert, and Friedrich Schneider (2007), "Was denken Deutsche Okonomen? Eine empirische Auswertung einer Internetbefragung unter den Mitgliddern des Vereins für Socialpolitik im Sommer 2006", *Perspektiven der Wirtschaftspolitik*, **8**(4), 359–77.

House, Bret, Sharada Weir, and Marcel Fafchamp (2002), "Getting a Job: Tips for Oxford DPhil Graduates", available at www.economics.ox.ac.uk/members/marcel.fafchamps/homepage/jobmarket.pdf (accessed 15 February 2009).

Kalaitzidakis, Pantelis, Theofanis P. Mamuneas, and Thanasis Stengos (1999), "European Economics: An Analysis Based on Publication in the Core Journals", *European Economic Review*, **43**(4–6), 1150–68.

Kalaitzidakis, Pantelis, Theofanis P. Mamuneas, and Thanasis Stengos (2003), "Rankings of Academic Journals and Institutions in Economics", *Journal of the European Economic Association*, **1**(6), 1346–66.

Kirman, Alan and Mogens Dahl (1994), "Economic Research in Europe", *European Economic Review*, **38**(3), 505–22.

Klamer, Arjo and David Colander (1990), *The Making of an Economist*, Boulder, CO: Westview Press.

Kolm, Serge-Christophe (1988), "Economics in Europe and the US", *European Economic Review*, **32**(1), January, 207–12.

Krueger, Anne O. et al. (1991), "Report of the Commission on Graduate Education in Economics", *Journal of Economic Literature*, **29**(3), September, 1035–53.

Kyklos (1995), Special Issue: Is There a European Economics?, **48**(2), 185–343.

Levitt, Steven D. and Stephen J. Dubner (2005), *Freakonomics: A Rogue Economist Explores the Hidden Side of Everything*, London: Allen Lane.

Mueller, Dennis (1995), "American and European Economists", *Kyklos*, **48**(2), 251–5.

Neary, Peter, James Mirrlees, and Jean Tirole (2003), "Evaluating Economics Research in Europe: An Introduction", *Journal of the European Economics Association*, **1**(6), December, 1239–49.

Portes, Richard (1987), "Economics in Europe", *European Economic Review*, **31**(6), August, 1329–40.

Puu, Tönu (2006), *Arts, Sciences, and Economics: A Historical Safari*, Berlin: Springer.

Rosser, J. Barkley, Jr., Richard P.F. Holt, and David Colander (2010), *European Economics at a Crossroad*, Cheltenham, UK and Northampton, MA, USA: Edward Elgar, forthcoming.

Salmon, Pierre (1995), "Three Conditions for Some Distinctiveness in the Contribution of Europeans to Economics", *Kyklos*, **48**(2), 279–87.

Stock, Wendy A. and W. Lee Hansen (2004), "Ph.D. Program Learning and Job Demands: How Close Is the Match?", *American Economic Review*, **94**(2) 266–71.

Thursby, Jerry (2000), "What Do We Say About Ourselves and What Does it Mean? Yet Another Look at Economics Department Research", *Journal of Economic Literature*, **38**(2), 383–404.

Index

academic research economists, job
  prospects
  in Bocconi interviews 98, 99, 103–4
  in LSE interviews 61–2, 77
  in Oxford interview 118, 119, 127
  in Pompeu Fabra interview 88, 89
  in quantitative results of European
    survey compared to US 11
  in Stockholm School of Economics
    interviews 111, 114
  US graduate economic programs
    25–6
advisory economists *see* government
  advisers; policy advisers
age of students, in making of a
  European economist survey 8
agreement of economists on
  fundamental issues 13, 111,
  114–15
analytical skills 32, 33, 34, 35, 36
applied econometrics 134
applied micro 75–6, 86, 87
applied policy 4, 21, 26, 61, 143,
  147–51, 158
Austrian school of economics 95, 101,
  108

Bank of England 63, 64, 142
behavioral economics
  in Bocconi interviews 94–5, 98, 101
  in LSE interviews 65, 66, 71, 72, 76
  in Oxford interview 123, 125
  in Stockholm School of Economics
    interviews 108, 112, 113
Bewley, Truman 6
Bocconi, Università
  and global economics 142
  interview 1 91–9
  interview 2 100–104
  in LSE interviews 62
Bonn, Universität 9, 16–19

books 74, 92, 120, 121, 146, 147, 172
bureaucratic institutional structure 43,
  44, 46, 97, 99

Cambridge controversy 137
Cambridge University 62, 137
central banks 15, 18, 63, 64, 88, 111,
  142
classes, structure of, in Pompeu Fabra
  interview 81–2
  see also typical day
classical economics 108, 109
COGEE 24–5
Colander, David 3, 4, 6, 25, 27, 145,
  164, 171, 172
Common European Educational Policy
  3, 8
communication inability 48, 49, 51,
  53, 55
communication skills 32, 33, 34, 35,
  36, 37
comparative economic systems 10
competition
  dislikes about graduate economic
    program, in qualitative results
    of European survey 43, 45, 46
  European graduate economic
    programs 141, 154, 171
  job markets, in quantitative results
    of European survey 20
  in market-based research solution
    for European economics 159
  in Pompeu Fabra interview 90
  publication in US graduate
    economic programs 23
  stressfulness in quantitative results
    of European survey compared
    to US 12, 93
  in US economic programs 23, 93
conflict of course and personal
  interests 12, 17